Bridal Crafts

Bridal Crafts

*Beautiful ideas for a special
wedding day*

Lucinda Ganderton

APPLE

A QUARTO BOOK

Published by the Apple Press
The Old Brewery
6 Blundell Street
London N7 9BH

A catalogue record for this book is available
from the British Library

ISBN 1-85076-917-6

This book was designed and produced by
Quarto Publishing plc
The Old Brewery
6 Blundell Street
London N7 9BH

Senior editor Michelle Pickering
Senior art editor Julie Francis
Copy editor Pat Pierce
Designer Liz Brown
Illustrator Elsa Godfrey
Photographers Ian Howes, David Sherwin
Models Anna Marsdon, Anna Parker
Prop buyers Zoë Holtermann, Maureen Kane
Art director Moira Clinch
Editorial director Pippa Rubinstein

Typeset by Central Southern Typesetters, Eastbourne, UK
Manufactured by Universal Graphics Pte Ltd, Singapore
Printed by Star Standard Industries (Pte) Ltd, Singapore

Contents

Introduction 6
Countdown to the wedding 7

Early Preparations
Lasting impressions 12
Albums of love 14
Box of delights 16
Lacy coat hanger 18
Beauty basket 20
Gorgeous gifts 22

Bridal Trousseau
Heirloom sampler 28
Sweetheart sachet 30
Love-birds pillow 32
A token of love 34
Sweet dreams 36

The Wedding Party
A token of affection 40
Beaded hat pin 42
Hat trick 44
Posy hair decoration 48
Beautiful doll 50
Victorian cornucopia 54
Cinderella slippers 56
Circlet of flowers 58
Ring bearer style 60
Bear essentials 62

Final Countdown
For the groom 66
Romantic ring pillow 68
Jeweled shoe clips 70
Good luck garter 72
Elegant tiara 74
Crowning glory 76
Everlasting bouquet 78
Bridal bag 80

Reception
Rose confetti box 86
Center of attention 88
Bonbonnières 90
Perfect place settings 92
Wedding cake tablecloth 94

Treasured Memories
Picture of happiness 98
Wedding dress box 100
LeMoyne star sachet 102
Drawstring shoe bag 104
Keepsake box 106
Découpage souvenir tray 108

Techniques & Templates
Basic sewing kit 110
Sewing techniques 110
Sewing stitches 111
Embroidery stitches 112
Templates 113

Index 126
Credits 128

Introduction

Every wedding is a unique occasion, full of hope and promise for the future. It is a ceremony of joy, which not only involves the bride and groom, but also joins together their friends and relatives in mutual celebration. Whether you are planning your own big day, or helping to arrange a marriage within the family, make it even more memorable by creating your own innovative gifts and accessories to add an unmistakably individual touch.

This book is designed to make the marriage preparations a time of great fun and creativity, which all your immediate circle will wish to join in. There is something here for everyone, and the inspirational bridal craft ideas are tailored to suit a variety of skills. Some can easily be completed in a spare afternoon, while others will involve many hours of love and care. There are items for the bride to sew for herself, her bridesmaids and ring bearer, or as thank-you presents for her closest friends, along with personal, romantic gifts that a devoted grandmother or the youngest cousin can make.

You will find fresh interpretations of old traditions and love tokens – a lucky lace garter, a flower-trimmed ring pillow, a stunning silk bouquet – and exciting contemporary craft ideas from leading designers. All are fully illustrated with clear step-by-step photographs, and accompanied by detailed instructions and easy-to-use templates. The methods featured cover popular needlecrafts such as ribbon weaving, embroidery, and appliqué, side-by-side with practical techniques including bead work, paper craft, stenciling, and découpage.

Depending on scale and formality, the actual organization of a wedding can take an average of six months. "Countdown to the Wedding" indicates when to undertake the various preparations and just when to start on the associated projects, beginning with the invitations and ending with a keepsake box to store precious souvenirs. By planning well ahead you can make sure that the day will pass smoothly and happily. It is, however, essential to know how much money you have to spend before you start making any arrangements, as costs can easily spiral. Allocate a sum for all the main items – reception, wedding dress, transportation, and so on –

and keep to it. The bride and groom should make all the major decisions together, and make sure that their families remain informed and involved throughout.

At the outset, you may well feel overwhelmed by the number of options open to you. Allow plenty of time to make your choices and avoid the feeling of being rushed. Compare notes with friends and relatives who have recently married, then research and read all the books and magazines you can before you decide on the details.

To make a really dramatic and stylish impact, the visual aspect of the wedding ceremony and reception, including flowers, dresses, and the bridegroom's outfit, should be considered from the outset. Build up your own resource of ideas and images by collecting a range of color swatches, fabric samples, lace, and ribbons, together with photographs and articles. Keep them filed in a large loose-leaf binder, and add your own sketches, notes, and thoughts. This can be used as an invaluable source book when you start on the projects, and will insure that they fit in with the overall color and design scheme.

The ideas in the following chapters will help you to add your own originality and inspiration to the wedding festivities, making it a day to remember forever.

Countdown to the Wedding

Once the engagement has been announced and the wedding date set, an exciting roller coaster of events moves into action. There are many etiquette books and formal planners available to guide you through the inevitable maze of organization, but this monthly countdown gives an easy-to-follow overview of what will be involved in the coming months. Treat the following as a list of ingredients, and to make your own wedding an individual event, pick out just the items that you wish to include. Don't feel constrained by tradition – the options are limited only by your own imagination!

6 MONTHS TO GO

- *Decide on the Ceremony*
Depending on your beliefs, the ceremony may be religious or civil, formal or informal.

- *Fix the Wedding Date*
This will depend on availability, so plan well in advance. Remember that popular locations quickly become booked up at weekends and during the summer months.

- *Book the Ceremony*
This may be held at a church, chapel, synagogue, register office, or other special location. Discuss any preparations – announcements, license, or counseling – with the relevant officials.

- *Book the Reception*
Decide now on the scale and timing. Will it be held in the same location as the service, at a nearby hotel, or a hired hall? Do you prefer a formal lunch, simple buffet, or a full-scale evening party? Start thinking about music, which could range from a rock band or disc jockey to a classic string quartet.

5 MONTHS TO GO

- *Decide on the Attendants*
They will be selected from among your closest friends and family, and depending on the formality of the wedding, may include a matron of honor, bridesmaids, flower girl, best man, groomsmen, ushers, and ring bearer.

- *Draw up a Guest List*
Friends, colleagues, and relatives, both distant and close, will share your day, but check with both your families so that no one is left out.

- *Talk to Caterers*
Now is the time to look at sample menus and discuss costs for food and drink, whether you will have in-house catering or will supply your own food.

- *Choose your Flowers*
These include the bride's bouquet, posies, flower baskets, corsages, and boutonnieres, along with decorations for the ceremony and reception. Talk over your ideas with a florist and make a provisional booking. If you prefer to make ever-lasting silk arrangements, start now and store them carefully in a dust-free environment.

8

4 MONTHS TO GO

• *Choose your Wedding Dress*
Visit several suppliers before you make a final decision. The dress may be specially made, bought off the rack, or rented. Allow time for fittings and alterations, then, when it has been delivered, keep it on a padded hanger, covered with a dress bag. Once you have the dress, look at co-ordinating head-wear, veils, hats, and shoes, and plan to make your own accessories.

• *Buy the Wedding Rings*
Matching gold bands for the bride and groom can be kept safe in their own padded and embroidered jewelry box until the wedding. This is the time to sew a lace-and-satin pillow for the ring bearer to carry.

• *Arrange the Honeymoon*
Check now that both your passports are valid, then plan your dream holiday. Sew a frilly case to hold your new lingerie or negligée.

• *Organize the Invitations*
Order or start making the wedding stationery. Decide on the wording and check the printer's proofs carefully. Start addressing envelopes whenever you have a spare moment, to save time later.

• *Book the Photographer*
Look at the work of a few photographers and discuss your requirements for formal and candid shots. Decide how many prints you will need, and who you will send them to. Make an album and start your own collection of snapshots now, to make a complete record of your wedding.

3 MONTHS TO GO

• *Send out the Invitations*
It is helpful to include a map with the invitations so that the guests know exactly where to go. Keep a checklist of acceptances.

• *Register for Gifts*
Department stores and design shops usually offer an in-house service, which is convenient and prevents duplication of gifts. Select as wide a range of items as possible, starting at pocket-money prices for children. Let guests know where you are registered.

• *Book Accommodations*
Guests who are traveling some distance may need to stay in a local hotel, so finalize the guest list and then check on who will need overnight accommodations.

• *Decide on the Bridesmaids' Outfits*
For a co-ordinated look you may prefer different designs made up in the same fabric, or the same style dress for all of the bridesmaids. Make sure that whatever style you choose suits each individual, particularly if their ages vary. Their accessories – head-dresses, garlands, and shoes – can all be made or bought as soon as the dresses have been chosen.

2 MONTHS TO GO

• *Organize the Men's Formal Wear*
The groom, best man, and ushers will usually wear rented outfits. It is easiest for them to be fitted at the same shop, but if this is not possible, ask them all for their measurements and make the arrangements yourself. As a surprise for the groom, decorate a special vest for him to wear under his jacket.

• *Book Transportation*
Sort out the car rental now and book chauffeur-driven cars or limousines to take the wedding party to the ceremony. Hire a carriage and horses for a really romantic entrance.

• *Prepare Personal Gifts*
A bride can return tokens of some of the love she has been given by making presents for her friends and family. Children will love a "ring-bear" or bridesmaid rag doll, while others will treasure a token such as a lace handkerchief, hatpin, or framed picture. The bride's friends can now create unique trousseau items: samplers, pincushions, and scented sachets.

1 MONTH TO GO

• *Arrange Official Announcements*

These can be sent now to both national and local newspapers. Check the wording carefully before you send them out.

• *Order the Cake*

You may be lucky enough to have a relative who is keen on decorative icing, but if not, order the cake from the best baker you can find. If it is to be on show at the reception, make or buy a special tablecloth for the display table.

• *Decide on Place Settings*

Napkin rings and favor bags can be made now, along with named place cards for the reception tables.

• *Finalize Arrangements*

Confirm, in writing, all the bookings and arrangements made with the various professionals: caterers, photographers, florists, chauffeurs, and so on.

1 WEEK TO GO

• *Check all Outfits*

So that everyone will feel comfortable in unfamiliar clothing, collect all the rented wear and make sure it fits, check the attendants' outfits, and practice walking in your new shoes. You may have organized a full-scale rehearsal for this week if your wedding is to be a formal occasion.

• *Pack for your Honeymoon*

Organize your going-away clothes. Remember, your honeymoon is a great excuse for buying luxurious new outer- and under-wear.

• *Book Beauty Treatments*

A day at a health spa, with facial and massage, is an ideal way for the bride and her matron of honor to relax just before the big day. Make a booking for this week, and also an appointment with your favorite hair dresser. Take the tiara, veil, or garland along, for a trial run of a new style.

• *Be Indulgent*

If you are the bride-to-be, take time out to unwind, on your own or in the company of your best friends, so you do not feel exhausted by the time your big day finally arrives!

AFTER THE EVENT

• *Write Thank-you Letters*

Acknowledge wedding gifts as soon as they arrive, but there are bound to be special notes to write on your return from honeymoon. Hand-made cards or paper will make them even more personal.

• *Store your Mementos*

Arrange for your dress to be dry-cleaned, then make a decorative box to store it in. Collect together all your cards and place them in a keepsake box or scrap album.

9

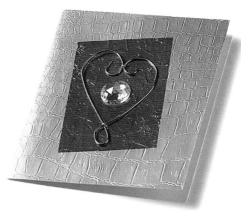

Early Preparations

The months before a wedding will be a busy time of great excitement for all involved, so the earlier you can start the organization, the lighter your workload will be. This applies whether you yourself are to be married, or if you are helping with the arrangements for a friend's or a family member's wedding. As soon as the date has been decided, stationery items such as cards, invitations, and albums, along with luxuries such as the cosmetic basket and ring box, can be made by or for the bride and stored in readiness for the day.

Lasting Impressions

This innovative and adaptable array of invitations, greeting cards, writing paper, and place cards will enable the bride and her circle to show just how much they care, by creating their own individual items of stationery.

Wedding-bells Greeting Card

CHOOSING YOUR MATERIALS

These projects need not be expensive to make – even the tiniest scraps of colored paper or foil saved from candy wrappings can be worked into your design. Check the range of decorative papers available at your local art supplier. They should also stock special pens and paints for drawing the motif or writing a special message. If you have a great many invitations to send, you may not wish to hand letter them all; to save time, the Bluebirds card incorporates an inner sheet that can be printed separately before it is assembled. Remember to follow the manufacturer's instructions when using spray adhesive.

YOU WILL NEED:

Metal ruler
★
Craft knife and cutting mat
★
8½ x 5½in (22 x 14cm) of textured white cardboard
★
Gold craft paint
★
Turquoise and pink relief paint
★
Silver glitter paint
★
Scrap of pink paper
★
Craft glue
★
PROJECT TIME *½ hour*

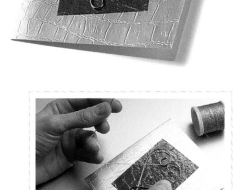

Jeweled-heart Greeting Card

YOU WILL NEED:

Metal ruler
★
Craft knife and cutting mat
★
5 x 8in (13 x 20cm) of textured gold cardboard
★
2½ x 3½in (6 x 9cm) of colored foil
★
Spray adhesive
★
10in (25cm) of gold wire
★
Needle and gold thread
★
Jewelry stone
★
Strong, clear adhesive
★
PROJECT TIME *½ hour*

Score the cardboard across the center and fold in half. Attach the foil to the front with spray adhesive. Bend the wire into a heart shape as shown. Thread the needle with a double length of thread and catch the heart to the front of the cardboard with a few stitches. Glue the jewelry stone inside the heart.

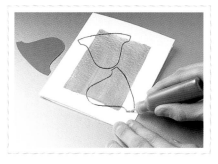

Score the cardboard across the center and fold in half. Paint a gold rectangle onto the front of the cardboard, leaving an unpainted frame ¾in (2cm) wide. Leave to dry, then following the design given in the Templates section, draw two bells over the gold area. Run a line of turquoise relief paint along the outlines. Add further details with pink relief and silver glitter paints. Cut two small hearts from pink paper and glue inside the bells.

Bluebirds-of-happiness Invitation

YOU WILL NEED:

Metal ruler

★

Craft knife and cutting mat

★

Sheet of white patterned gift wrap

★

Sheet of white cardboard

★

Sheet of fine white paper

★

Blue paper

★

Spray adhesive

★

Gold pen

★

20in (50cm) of fine gold cord

★

Hole punch

★

PROJECT TIME ½ hour

Mount the gift wrap onto cardboard with spray adhesive and cut two 5½ x 4in (14 x 10cm) rectangles. Use the design from the Templates section to cut two birds from blue paper. Glue them to one of the rectangles and draw the details in gold. Cut a 5 x 3in (13 x 8cm) rectangle of white paper. Sandwich this between the front and back pieces so that the left edges are level. Punch two holes along the left edge and lace together with cord. Fasten into a bow, then trim and knot the ends.

Bird-of-paradise Place Card

YOU WILL NEED:

Metal ruler

★

Craft knife and cutting mat

★

Sheet of thin cardboard

★

Sheet of textured pink paper

★

Spray adhesive

★

Sheet of textured white cardboard

★

Dressmaker's pin

★

6in (15cm) of fine gold wire

★

Strong, clear adhesive

★

PROJECT TIME ½ hour

Attach the paper to the cardboard with spray adhesive and cut a 3½ x 4in (9 x 10cm) rectangle. Score lengthwise along the center and fold in half. Using the design given in the Templates section, cut a bird from white cardboard. Pierce a hole at the eye and tail tip with a pin. Bend the wings forward gently, then thread the wire through the tail hole. Bend it upward and coil the ends. Glue the bird to the top right corner of the place card.

Thank-you Paper

YOU WILL NEED:

Metal ruler

★

Textured blue writing paper

★

White ribbon rose

★

6in (15cm) of fine gold wire

★

Needle and sewing thread

★

PROJECT TIME ½ hour

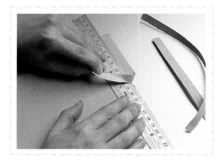

To give a deckle finish to the paper, hold a ruler ½in (1cm) inside each edge and tear the paper along each side, pulling the strip toward you. Bend the wire in half and coil the ends. Attach to the top-left corner of the paper with a few stitches and sew the rose on top.

Albums of Love

A jewel-bedecked cover will turn an ordinary photograph album into a very special keepsake. If made well in advance, the bride can use it for all the snapshots that are taken during the events leading up to the wedding, as well as pictures from the day itself.

CHOOSING YOUR MATERIALS

This informal bead embroidery shows up to best effect on a textured background, so look for interesting fabrics for the cover. Crushed velvet, pleated organza, and figured silk could all be used, along with a matching satin for the lining. A blank-paged book in a complementary color scheme makes a good companion for the album. The service and reception are bound to pass in a whirl of activity, so create a personal record of the day by asking each guest to write a message within its pages.

YOU WILL NEED:

Photograph album
★
Cream fabric
★
Medium-weight batting
★
Cream lining fabric
★
Gold and crystal jewelry stones
and beads
★
1yd (90cm) of 1½in (4cm) wide
striped gold ribbon
★
Matching sewing thread
★
Sewing machine
★
Basic sewing kit
★
PROJECT TIME *5 hours*

You could also make albums to celebrate other important family events, such as birthdays, christenings, or wedding anniversaries.

1 Cut a rectangle each of fabric, batting, and lining large enough to wrap around the album, plus 1in (2.5cm) all around. With right sides outward, pin the fabric to the batting with the lining underneath. Machine quilt the layers with irregular, but pleasing, rows of straight stitch, worked parallel to the short edges. Wrap the cover around the album to check the fit. Trim the allowance to ½in (15mm) and stitch close to the edge. On one half of the cover, sew the jewelry stones and beads in clusters along the quilting lines, keeping them within 1in (2.5cm) of the edge.

14

2 Snip the ribbon in half, and pin one end of each piece to the center of each short edge. Cut two 4in (10cm) strips of lining, the length of the short edge, to make the facings. Neaten one long edge with a narrow double hem. Cut a rectangle of lining the same size as the cover.

3 With right sides together and raw edges matching, pin the facings to each end of the cover. Pin, then baste the lining on top. Stitch together, ⅜in (1cm) from the outer edge, leaving a 3in (8cm) opening along one side. Clip the seam allowance across the corners, then trim back the batting.

4 Turn the cover right side out, and press lightly. Close the gap with slip stitch. Slip the album into the cover, so that the facings hold it in place. Tie the ribbons in a bow, and trim the loose ends into chevrons. Make a coordinating message book in the same way.

Albums of Love

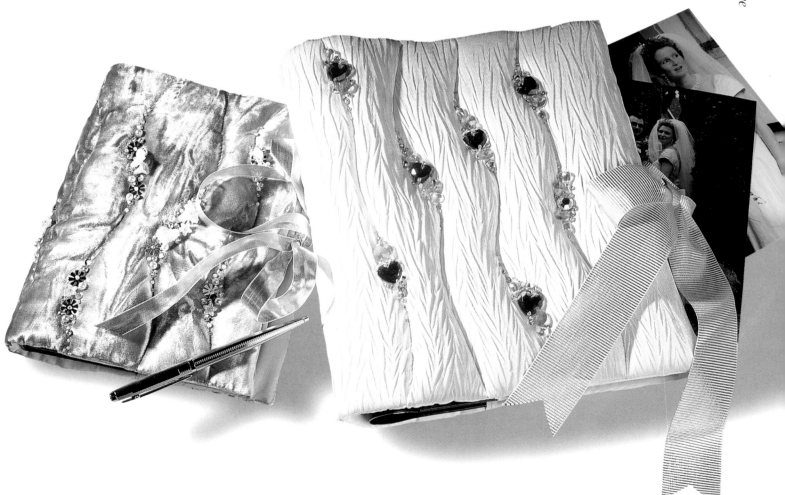

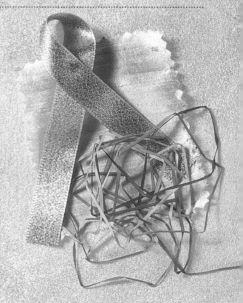

Box of Delights

This heart-shaped box, decorated with ribbon embroidery and gold initials, is the perfect place to keep the bride and groom's rings before the wedding day, and will make a charming container for their favorite jewelry in the future.

16

YOU WILL NEED:

6in (15cm) heart-shaped
cardboard box
★
18in (45cm) of 45in (115cm) wide
silk douppioni
★
Soft pencil
★
Embroidery frame or hoop
★
3yds (270cm) each of: yellow gold,
bright yellow, dark blue, medium
green, emerald green, and yellow
green embroidery ribbon
★
Stranded yellow embroidery
thread
★
Gold thread
★
10in (25cm) of medium-weight
batting
★
1yd (90cm) of 8in (20cm) wide
heavyweight iron-on interfacing
★
Double-sided adhesive tape
★
Craft glue
★
20in (50cm) of ¹⁄₂in (15mm) wide
gold ribbon
★
Matching sewing thread
★
Basic sewing kit
★
PROJECT TIME 8 *hours*

CHOOSING YOUR MATERIALS

Stitching with special fine silk ribbon is no more complicated than working with thread or wool, and produces attractive three-dimensional results. It needs to be worked onto a fabric with a firm weave, such as the silk douppioni used here, and it is important not to pull the stitches too tightly as you embroider. The elegant copperplate letters are sewn in split stitch, using gold thread. A full alphabet is given in the Techniques & Templates section, along with detailed instructions for working the stitches.

Box of Delights

1 Cut a 9in (23cm) square of silk. Draw the design from the Templates section onto the fabric. Add your chosen initials either side of the ampersand (&). Stretch the fabric in an embroidery frame. Stitch the leaves in lazy daisy stitch, working the clusters in different shades of green. Work the rosebuds by stitching a yellow lazy daisy stitch into an emerald green one.

2 Stitch a five-pointed star for each rose with two strands of embroidery thread. Bring a length of yellow ribbon up in the center of the star and begin to weave the ribbon under and over the thread. Allow the ribbon to twist softly and continue until all the thread is covered. Take the needle back through and tie off.

3 As you work around the heart, sew clusters of French knots in blue and yellow to fill in the gaps between the leaves and roses. Using the gold thread, stitch around the outline of the letters using split stitch. Fill in the solid areas with rows of split stitch.

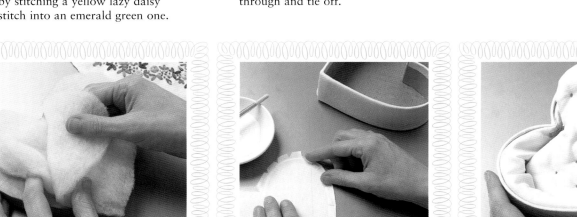 

4 Cut three graduated layers of batting to fit the box lid. Fix in place with double-sided tape, keeping the largest heart at the top. Attach double-sided tape around the rim of the lid. Trim the embroidered panel 1in (2.5cm) from the embroidery. Snip into the seam allowance at the top of the heart and stretch the fabric over the batting and down onto the tape. Glue gold ribbon around the outside rim.

5 Cover the outside of the box with bias strips of silk. Use double-sided tape to secure the raw edges and to hold the fabric in place along the inside edge. Cut two interfacing hearts for the base of the box and the inside lid and iron onto silk. Trim the seam allowance to ¼in (6mm) and notch. Spread adhesive around the edge of the interfacing and fold the seam allowance over. Glue the covered hearts in position.

6 For the padded lining, cut a strip of interfacing to fit each side of the box and a heart for the base. Cut out and baste two layers of batting to each shape, then cover with silk cut on the bias grain, adding a ½in (15mm) seam allowance. Baste the silk in place, with the seam allowances taken to the back of the pieces. With double-sided tape, stick the side strips inside the box and slip stitch the joins. Finish with a ribbon bow at the top. Quilt the heart by working rows of blue French knots through all the layers. Fit inside the box.

Lacy Coat Hanger

*This flower- and lace-trimmed coat hanger,
complete with a matching scented heart sachet,
may appear to be an extravagance, but, happily,
it also has a very practical use.*

CHOOSING YOUR MATERIALS

The bridal gown may arrive many weeks before the wedding day
and must be stored carefully. A padded hanger will help to keep
the bodice and shoulders in shape and protect the gown from
creasing. Ask the dressmaker for remnants of fabric to make a
hanger to match the gown itself, or choose this nostalgic
combination of dusky pink satin and cream lace. The heart-
shaped sachet can be filled with potpourri or batting scented
with the bride's favorite fragrance.

YOU WILL NEED:

Wooden coat hanger

★

16 x 20in (40 x 50cm) of batting

★

8 x 36in (20 x 90cm) of
colored satin

★

6 x 20in (15 x 50cm) of
embroidered net

★

1yd (90cm) of 3in (10cm) wide
lace edging

★

16in (40cm) of ½in (15mm)
wide lace

★

Fabric flower and leaves

★

Potpourri or batting

★

Matching sewing thread and
contrasting basting thread

★

Basic sewing kit

★

PROJECT TIME *3 hours*

1 Cut one 6in (15cm) and one
10in (25cm) bias strip from
satin, and make into rouleaux
(see Techniques & Templates).
Turn the raw edge at one end of the
shorter strip to the wrong side and
slip stitch to neaten. Slip the tube
onto the hook and secure at the
base by stitching over the hanger.

2 Fold the batting in half widthwise and cut along the fold to
within 1in (2.5cm) of the edge.
Wrap it around the hanger and sew
in place with large over stitches.

3 Cut a 6 x 20in (15 x 50cm)
rectangle from satin, and snip a
small hole in the center. Press
under ¼in (5mm) along one long
edge. Place the satin over the hook,
and wrap it around the hanger. Pin,
then slip stitch, the folded edge
over the raw edge. Trim and sew
down the two ends.

4 Press under ½in (15mm) along one long edge of the embroidered net, and then cut a small hole in the center. Fit and pin the net over the hanger, as for the satin. Next, neaten the lace edging by sewing a narrow double hem at each short end.

5 Run a gathering thread along the top edge of the lace edging and draw it up to the same length as the hanger. Fix in place by tucking the gathers under the folded edge of the net, re-pinning as you go. Slip stitch in place. Trim and stitch down the two ends.

6 Using the design in the Templates section as a guide, cut out two heart shapes from the remaining satin. Pin and stitch together with right sides facing, ⅓in (8mm) from the edge. Leave a 1in (2.5cm) gap along one straight side, and clip the curves. Turn right sides out, fill with batting or petals, and slip stitch the gap. Gather the narrow lace to fit, and slip stitch around the outside edge of the heart.

7 Fold the second rouleau in half to make a loop, and sew to the top of the heart. Sew on the leaves and flower so that they conceal the raw ends. Secure the sachet to the hanger with a few stitches.

Beauty Basket

Every bride should be pampered on the day of her wedding, in ways both large and small. This country-style basket is the ideal place for her to keep her perfume and cosmetics while she and her attendants prepare for the ceremony.

CHOOSING YOUR MATERIALS

By adding a flowered cotton lining and a few coats of paint, a plain wicker basket can be transformed into a pretty bedroom accessory. Use acrylic craft colors to paint the border, picking out two dominant shades from the fabric itself, then rub down the basket to give it a subtly antiqued finish. The instructions are for a basket measuring 22in (55cm) around the base; if you are going to line a larger version, scale up the quantity of fabric.

YOU WILL NEED:

Round or oval wicker basket
★
Acrylic craft paints and medium paintbrush
★
Wire wool or fine sandpaper
★
Paper and pencil
★
10in (25cm) square of plain cotton fabric
★
20 x 36in (50 x 90cm) of printed cotton fabric
★
1yd (90cm) of 3in (8cm) wide broderie-anglaise lace edging with insertion slots
★
1yd (90cm) of ¾in (2cm) wide broderie-anglaise trim
★
1yd (90cm) of ⅜in (1cm) wide satin ribbon
★
Safety pin
★
Matching sewing thread
★
Sewing machine
★
Basic sewing kit
★
PROJECT TIME *3 hours*

1 Sand down the basket to remove any rough edges. Paint with a base coat of white acrylic, making sure that it reaches into all the crevices. Paint the outer rim in bands of two colors, and when completely dry, rub lightly with sandpaper or wire wool.

2 Make a template for the base of the lining by drawing around the basket onto a sheet of paper. Add on ½in (15mm) all around the outline, then cut out. Fold into quarters, and trim to make the shape symmetrical. Place the template inside the basket to check the fit. Cut one base from plain cotton fabric, then fold into quarters and notch the creases.

3 Cut the floral fabric in half lengthwise. Fold each strip into a loop with right sides facing, and stitch together ½in (15mm) from the short edges. Press the seams flat. Fold both pieces into four, and notch the creases along one edge. Sew a series of gathering threads between the notches. With the right side facing inward, pin one loop to the base to make the inner lining, matching the notches. Draw up the gathering threads to fit, then pin and stitch together.

4 With wrong sides together, join the ends of the lace to form a loop. Trim the seam to ⅛in (3mm), open out, and press. Fold the lace right sides together and press the seam flat. Stitch a second seam, enclosing the raw edges, then press the seam to one side. With the right side facing inward, pin the straight edge of the lace loop to the right side of the inner lining. Pin the outer lining over the lace so that the right side faces inward and the seams are matched up with the inner piece. Stitch through all three layers, ½in (15mm) from the edge.

5 Turn back the outer lining, and press the seam. Sew the broderie-anglaise trim over the join between the fabric and lace edging.

6 Turn under the raw edge of the outer lining and baste. Gather this edge to fit the base, as before, and stitch down. Place the completed lining inside the basket and pin. Sew in place with a double length of thread, passing the needle through the basket weave to the inside of the lining.

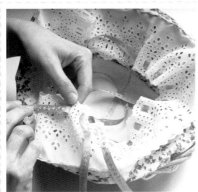

7 Fasten the safety pin to one end of the satin ribbon and thread through the insertion slots around the lace edging. Trim the ends of the ribbon neatly, then draw up, and tie into a bow.

Gorgeous Gifts

Wedding presents are chosen with love and care, and you can make your gift for the new couple even more special with one of these clever ideas for gift wrapping.

CHOOSING YOUR MATERIALS

Most household items are bought in their own special packaging, which is easy to cover. Other gifts, however, may be awkwardly shaped, and are best wrapped in protective tissue and packed inside a ready-made presentation box. These come in many shapes: oval, round, hexagonal, and square. Instead of using an expensive printed paper, try embellishing a plain sheet yourself, or hunt for gauzy fabrics such as net, organza, and voile, with which to wrap your gift. Finish with a specially made gift tag, and a spray of silk or even fresh flowers as the final touch.

22

Rose and Organza Box

YOU WILL NEED:

Square gold gift box
★
Gold metallic organza
★
1yd (90cm) of 1½in (4cm) wide
pink wire-edged ribbon
★
Pink silk rose
★
PROJECT TIME *½ hour*

1 Cut a large square of organza, and lay it centrally over the open gift box. Put the lid on top, sandwiching the fabric, and lift the fabric to the top of the box.

2 Tie the ribbon around the fabric in a bow. Slip the stem of the rose behind the ribbon, and trim the trailing ends of the ribbon into chevrons.

Box of Pretty Pinks

YOU WILL NEED:

Oval gift box

★

Pink organza

★

Four 1yd (90cm) lengths of
⅛in (3mm) wide ribbon in
shades of pink

★

Spray of cream silk flowers

★

PROJECT TIME ½ *hour*

Cut an oval of organza large
enough to wrap completely around
the box, with an 8in (20cm) frill at
the top. Stand the box on the
organza and pull up the fabric
around it, so that the gathers lie
slightly off-center. Tie the ribbons
in a bow around the fabric and
trim the trailing ends. Slip a spray
of flowers behind the bow.

*Box of
Pretty Pinks*

*Rose and
Organza Box*

Butterfly Box

YOU WILL NEED:

Rectangular gift box

★

Gold gift wrap

★

Silver costume jewelry stones

★

Relief paints in silver and two shades of pink

★

2yds (180cm) of pink cord

★

String of tiny pink pearls

★

Textured pink paper

★

Thin cardboard

★

Gold and silver pens

★

Strong, clear adhesive

★

Spray adhesive

★

PROJECT TIME ½ hour

Gorgeous Gifts

1 Wrap the box with gold paper. Tie it up with pink cord and finish in a bow. Glue jewelry stones at random on the paper. Apply a swirl of pink relief paint around each stone. Leave to dry. Tie a string of pearls to the bow.

2 To make the gift tag, mount the pink paper onto cardboard with spray adhesive. Use the design given in the Templates section to cut out a butterfly. Draw in the details with a pencil, then redraw with metallic pens and relief paint. Leave to dry, then score along the broken lines and fold the wings upward. Glue on jewelry stones. The butterfly can be lightly glued to the gift after the message is written.

Shells & Bells Box

Butterfly Box

Cupid's Heart Boxes

Shells & Bells Box

YOU WILL NEED:

Round gift box

★

3⅓yds (300cm) of 1½in (4cm) wide embroidered cream wire-edged ribbon

★

Shell-shaped sequins

★

Gold cardboard and hole punch

★

10in (25cm) of ⅛in (3mm) wide satin ribbon

★

Strong, clear adhesive

★

PROJECT TIME ½ hour

1 Cut a 2½yd (230cm) length of wire-edged ribbon. Fold into 10in (25cm) deep concertina pleats. Snip through the wire edge on each side of the ribbon at the center point, and tie the remaining ribbon around the middle of the pleats.

2 Place the pleats on top of the lid, pull the two ribbon ends to the inside of the lid, and glue in position. Spread out the loops and cut the trailing ends into chevrons. Glue shell-shaped sequins at random on the box.

3 Use the design in the Templates section to cut two bells from gold cardboard for the gift tag. Glue a shell-shaped sequin to each bell. Punch a hole at the top, and thread onto fine ribbon. Tie to the bow.

Cupid's Heart Boxes

YOU WILL NEED:

2 different-sized square gift boxes

★

Pink tissue paper

★

2yds (180cm) of gold cord

★

Gold relief paint

★

Ornamental gilt cherub

★

Strong, clear adhesive

★

PROJECT TIME ½ hour

Wrap the two boxes neatly with pink tissue paper. Place the small box on top of the large, and tie the two together with gold cord. Knot the ends of the cord. Draw a scattering of tiny hearts on the packages with a gold relief pen. Leave to dry, then glue on the cherub.

Bridal Trousseau

"Trousseau" is an old French word that literally translates as "little bundle" – the household goods and dowry items that a young woman took to her new home as she embarked on married life. The term is now used to include the souvenirs that are given by her close friends as a symbol of their love and best wishes for the future. These romantic and traditional keepsakes are just for the bride herself – and are more personal than the wedding presents that she and her husband will receive. Make her an individual gift using your own special skills or favorite needlecraft technique.

Heirloom Sampler

The thought, time, and patience that go into creating a traditional cross-stitch sampler make it a real labor of love. This present will be much appreciated by the bride and groom, and treasured as an heirloom.

CHOOSING YOUR MATERIALS

To personalize your sampler, a complete upper and lower case alphabet is given with the chart in the Techniques & Templates section, so that you can embroider a personal message, along with the couple's initials and the date of their wedding. Draw this on graph paper first, to work out the amount of space it will take. The design is stitched in two strands of embroidery thread on 28-count even-weave linen, but you may prefer to use 14-count cross-stitch cloth. For a really professional finish, stretch the finished piece onto mountboard before it is framed.

28

YOU WILL NEED:

16 x 18in (40 x 45cm) of 28-count even-weave linen in antique white

★

Contrasting basting thread

★

Size 24 tapestry needle

★

1 skein each of stranded embroidery thread: dark (2 skeins), medium, and light blue; very pale blue; dark emerald green; and yellow for French knots

★

12 x 14in (30 x 36cm) of mountboard

★

Pencil and ruler

★

Strong thread, such as quilting cotton

★

Basic sewing kit

★

PROJECT TIME *20 hours*

If you do not have time to stitch the complete design, the heart motif can be worked on its own to make an equally effective small picture or pincushion.

1 Neaten the edge of the linen with buttonhole stitch or a machine zigzag to prevent it from fraying. Using a dark thread, mark the center point by basting two intersecting guidelines across the middle of the fabric.

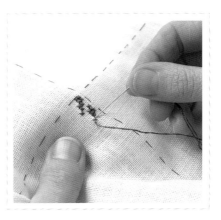

2 The chart in Techniques & Templates shows where to use each color. Each square on the chart represents one cross stitch worked over two threads of linen. Thread the needle with two strands of thread and bring it through to the right side of the linen. Leave a 2in (5cm) tail at the back and stitch it down as you sew. Do not carry the thread between motifs or it will show through, but finish each one individually by sewing the end under a few threads and snipping neatly. Once the cross stitch has been completed, work French knots in the flower centers, which are represented by circles on the chart.

3 Press the finished piece of embroidery on the reverse side with a steam iron. Measure and mark the mid-point on each side of the mountboard. Lay the embroidery face down and line up the mid-point marks on the board with the basted guidelines.

4 Insert pins into the edge of the mountboard at the center points to hold the cloth in place. Working along the straight grain, insert more pins at 1in (2.5cm) intervals. Lace the edges together from side to side using a long length of strong thread. Join on any extra lengths of thread with a double knot. Fold in the corners and sew the top and bottom together in the same way.

5 Once completed, make the lacing taut by gently lifting one thread at a time the whole way across and finishing the ends off securely. Remove the basting thread. When you frame the embroidery, remember to use picture spacers to keep the glass away from the stitches.

Sweetheart Sachet

This sumptuous lace-and-bead heart is filled with dried flowers and fragrant herbs to bring the heady aroma of a summer garden to any room.

CHOOSING YOUR MATERIALS

A trousseau consists of both useful presents and long-remembered luxuries. A wedding is a good excuse to indulge yourself by creating lavish refinements, such as this scented heart-shaped sachet. Many florists and craft stores sell a variety of potpourri, but to make the gift even more special, why not collect petals, buds, and leaves from your own plants? Add a few drops of essential oil – rose, neroli, or lavender – and a sprinkling of powdered orris root to fix and intensify the scents.

YOU WILL NEED:

Tracing paper and pencil

★

8 x 10in (20 x 25cm) of lace fabric

★

10 x 18in (25 x 45cm) of dark pink satin or silk

★

Metallic copper and pearlized pink, cream, and green embroidery beads

★

1yd (90cm) of 2in (5cm) wide lace edging

★

12in (30cm) each of 1½in (4cm) and 3in (8cm) wide matching organza ribbon

★

Potpourri

★

Size 11 needle

★

Matching sewing thread and contrasting basting thread

★

Sewing machine

★

Basic sewing kit

★

PROJECT TIME *4 hours*

1 Draw and cut out the heart shape from Techniques & Templates. Using this as a pattern, cut two hearts from satin and one from lace. Pin, then baste one of the satin hearts to the back of the lace, matching the edges exactly.

2 Study the lace carefully and pick out interesting shapes and design details. Emphasize these by sewing on the beads, singly and in short rows. Make a decorative center for any flower shapes by sewing a loop of 8 pearlized beads around a darker metallic bead.

3 Run a gathering thread along the straight edge of the lace edging and draw it up to fit around the embroidered heart. Starting at the center top, pin the two together so that the gathers face toward the center. Distribute the fullness evenly as you pin. Machine stitch the lace down, ⅓in (1cm) from the edge.

4 Pin the second satin heart over the first, making sure that the lace edging does not get caught between them. Sew together, leaving a gap of 2in (5cm) along one straight edge. Stitch just inside the previous stitching line.

5 Trim back the seam allowances, then clip the point and the curves. Turn the heart right side out, and press the seam lightly with the tip of the iron. Fill the sachet with potpourri or dried herbs, then close the gap with slip stitch.

6 Fold the wide ribbon in half, and stitch to the top of the heart to form a hanging loop. Turn under the raw ends of the ribbon neatly when you sew it in place. Tie the narrow ribbon into a bow, and sew to the front of the sachet.

Love-Birds Pillow

In a tradition dating back to the cult of Venus, goddess of love, doves – the love-birds – have been thought of as bearers of good fortune. Reflecting ancient custom, this opulent pillow will bless any bride with good luck.

32

CHOOSING YOUR MATERIALS

It is considered a particularly good omen to spy a dove on your wedding morning, and a pair of white doves is also a favorite symbol for painting onto bridal chests. The two birds that decorate this velvet pillow are sewn by machine in gold and silver thread, but if you prefer to embroider by hand, the design could be interpreted in an outline stitch, such as chain or stem stitch. The choice of two shades of velvet as the background fabric adds a rich depth of texture, and this is offset by the silken cord which has been sewn around the edge of the cover.

YOU WILL NEED:

20 x 36in (50 x 90cm) of light pink velvet

★

5 x 13in (13 x 33cm) of dusky pink velvet

★

6 x 16in (15 x 40cm) each of silver and gold metallic organza

★

Silver and gold metallic embroidery threads

★

13in (33cm) of ½in (15mm) wide gold ribbon

★

70in (180cm) of furnishing cord

★

12 x 22in (30 x 55cm) pillow form

★

Tissue paper

★

Matching sewing thread and contrasting basting thread

★

Sewing machine

★

Basic sewing kit

★

PROJECT TIME *3 hours*

1 Cut a 13 x 19in (33 x 48cm) rectangle from the light pink velvet. With right sides together, join to the strip of dusky pink velvet ½in (15mm) from the edge. Draw the dove design from the Templates section onto tissue paper. Pin the tissue to the wrong side of the larger panel.

2 Pin the two pieces of organza to the right side of the panel, so that the gold organza covers one half of the rectangle and the silver organza covers the other half. Baste the three layers together.

3 Thread the sewing machine with silver thread. Working over the tissue paper, straight stitch over the pencil outline on the reverse of the silver organza. Sew around the shape three times. Change to gold thread and work the second bird in the same way.

4 When the stitching is complete, tear away the tissue paper. Turn the work over and, using sharp embroidery scissors, trim away the excess organza from around the lines of stitching.

5 Pin the ribbon over the seam between the two pieces of velvet. Sew down with a narrow zigzag. From the remaining velvet, cut two rectangles, measuring 13 x 18in (33 x 45cm) and 10 x 13in (25 x 33cm). Make a $\frac{1}{3}$in (1cm) double hem along one 13in (33cm) side on each piece. With right sides facing, pin the larger rectangle to one side of the pillow top with the neatened edge facing inward. Pin the smaller rectangle to the other side, in the same way. Stitch together around the outside edge, leaving a 1in (2.5cm) gap at one side. Clip the corners and turn right sides out.

6 Tuck one end of the cord into the gap and secure with a few stitches. Sew the cord in place around the seam line. Tuck the other end of the cord into the gap and stitch closed. Insert the pillow form.

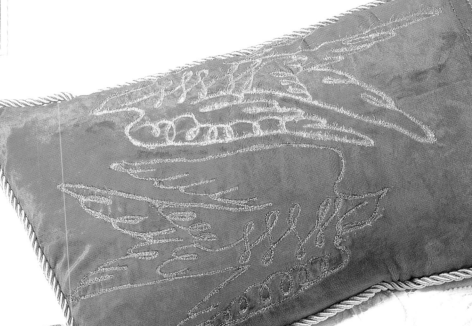

A Token of Love

Folk art pincushions were made throughout the nineteenth century, both as love-tokens and to commemorate family events such as weddings and christenings. This brightly beaded flower basket will inspire you to continue the tradition.

CHOOSING YOUR MATERIALS

The basic pincushion, which is made from silk douppioni, must be stuffed firmly to give it weight and to hold the pins securely in position. Like the originals, it has been filled with sawdust, which has been packed solidly to give the characteristic pointed corners. A mixture of brass and steel pins, metallic and translucent beads, and tiny flat silver sequins are used to outline the design, with a few larger gold sequins and diamantés to add highlights. A special Victorian-style alphabet is included in the Techniques & Templates section, so you can personalize the pincushion with the bride and groom's initials.

34

YOU WILL NEED:

9 x 15in (23 x 38cm) of cream silk tussore

★

Tracing paper

★

Black fiber-tipped pen

★

Masking tape

★

Chalk pencil

★

Sawdust

★

Small metallic gold and bronze round beads

★

Small translucent gold and clear round beads

★

Three ⅜in (10mm) diameter flat diamantés with center holes

★

Three ¼in (6mm) diameter flat gold sequins

★

⅛in (3mm) diameter flat silver sequins

★

Brass lacemaking pins

★

Dressmaker's steel pins

★

1yd (90cm) of cream fringed edging

★

Clear nail polish

★

Matching sewing thread

★

Basic sewing kit

★

Sewing machine

★

PROJECT TIME *6 hours*

A Token of Love

1 Transfer the flower basket from the Templates section onto tracing paper, using a black pen to give a strong outline. Cut the silk into two rectangles, each measuring 7½ x 9in (19 x 23cm). Fix one piece centrally over the design with masking tape and trace over it carefully with a chalk pencil.

2 With right sides together, pin and stitch the two silk rectangles together, ½in (15mm) from the edge. Leave a 2in (5cm) gap in the center of one short edge. Press the unstitched seam allowance to the wrong side, then clip the corners and turn right sides out. Ease the corners into shape and fill the bag with sawdust. Pack it down until the pincushion is firm, then slip stitch the gap closed.

3 Pin one diamanté to the center of each flower. Outline the large rose and the two horizontal lines on the basket by pinning bronze beads along the chalk lines. Make sure that the beads lie closely and neatly together. Fix three gold sequins along the basket's center band, and a bronze bead at the points of each oval. Outline the basket and the oval band with metallic gold beads.

4 The hearts, stems, tendrils, and insides of the leaves are filled in with steel pins, placed next to each other so that the heads form a series of dots. Use small silver sequins for the leaf shapes, pinning each one in place with a brass pin.

5 The two outer roses are filled in with translucent gold beads, and their centers defined with circles of clear beads. Pin a sequin at the start and finish of each letter in the monograms, and then fill in the lines with pins.

6 Finish off by pinning the fringing around the edge of the pincushion. Start at one corner, and butt the two ends together. If the fringe is likely to fray, seal the cut edges with clear nail polish.

Sweet Dreams

A romantic silk negligée or lace-trimmed nightdress is an essential part of a bride's trousseau, and deserves its own special case in which to be taken away on honeymoon.

CHOOSING YOUR MATERIALS

A deep frill of crisp cotton lace and an old-world sprigged dress print are combined in this traditional version, which could also be used as a lingerie bag. Hand-covered buttons add the finishing touch. They are embroidered with dainty sprays of forget-me-nots and daisies, which, in the language of flowers, represent true love and beauty respectively.

2 Neaten each end of the lace edging with a narrow double hem. Run a gathering thread along the straight edge and draw up to 17in (42cm). Pin to the unstitched edge of the narrow floral strip, ½in (15mm) in from the sides. Distribute the gathers evenly.

YOU WILL NEED:

32 x 36in (80 x 90cm) of floral cotton fabric

★

19in (48cm) of 1½in (4cm) wide broderie-anglaise lace insertion

★

30in (75cm) of 3in (8cm) wide broderie-anglaise lace edging

★

6 x 10in (15 x 25cm) of white cotton fabric

★

Stranded embroidery thread in yellow, pale green, light blue, mauve, and pink

★

Five 1in (2.5cm) self-cover buttons

★

Matching sewing thread

★

Sewing machine

★

Basic sewing kit

★

PROJECT TIME *4 hours*

1 Cut the floral fabric into two rectangles, each measuring 18 x 32in (45 x 80cm), and then cut a ½in (4cm) strip from the end of one piece. This will be the top piece. With right sides together, sew the strip to the lace insertion, ¼in (5mm) from the edge. Sew the other side of the lace to the shorter rectangle and press the seam allowances toward the fabric.

3 With right sides facing, pin the lace-trimmed end of the top piece to one short end of the other floral rectangle, then pin along the two sides. Trim both pieces to the same length, then pin the remaining short end. Sew together, ½in (15mm) from the edge. Leave a 3in (8cm) gap along the undecorated short end. Clip the corners and turn right sides out, then slip stitch the gap closed. Press.

4 Make the bag by folding the lower 12in (30cm) toward the lace-trimmed end and pinning the sides together. Join each side with a narrow zigzag stitch, worked so that it overlaps the double edge.

5 Mark five circles onto white cotton fabric using the template supplied with the button kit. Using two strands of embroidery thread, stitch the flower motif onto each, following the design given in the Templates section. Vary the colors for each button, as desired. Make up the buttons according to the instructions supplied.

6 Sew the completed buttons securely at regular intervals along the broderie-anglaise strip. Fold the decorated edge over to the front of the case.

The
Wedding Party

As the big day draws near, the bride and groom will inevitably be at the center of events, so time during the two months preceding the ceremony should be spent concentrating on the other important members of the wedding party. There is something in this chapter for guests of all ages. The younger bridesmaids and ring bearers will be prepared for their roles with special outfits and new toys, while mothers, sisters, aunts, and "best friends" will also appreciate their own individual gift such as a handkerchief, barrette, or a new hat with a matching hat pin.

A Token of Affection

Every mother may shed a sentimental tear at her son or daughter's wedding, so it would be thoughtful to give her this fine linen handkerchief on the day itself as a token of thanks and love.

40

CHOOSING YOUR MATERIALS

Sew an edging of delicate cotton lace to a plain white square and appliqué the corners with motifs cut from long-hoarded fragments of old lace. Newly purchased lace can be given a softer, antique look by dipping it in a solution of tea until it reaches a warm cream shade. Make the handkerchief even more individual by adding embroidered detail – perhaps the couple's initials and the date of the wedding, or a special message.

YOU WILL NEED:

12in (30cm) square linen handkerchief with drawn-thread edge

★

60in (150cm) of 1½in (4cm) wide lace edging

★

Scraps of colored lace

★

Matching sewing thread

★

Basic sewing kit

★

PROJECT TIME *2 hours*

A Token of Affection

1 Leaving an overlap of 1in (2.5cm) at one corner, start stitching the lace to the edge of the handkerchief. Use a fine needle and sew with an unobtrusive slip stitch. Work to within ¼in (5mm) of the second corner, and finish off the sewing thread. Gather the next 3in (8cm) of the lace and draw up tightly. Stitch the gathers around the corner, then sew the next two sides in the same way.

2 When you are ¼in (5mm) away from the final corner, join the two loose ends of the lace, wrong sides together. Trim the seam to ⅛in (3mm), open out, and press. Fold the lace right sides together and press the seam flat. Stitch a second seam, enclosing the raw edges, then press the seam to one side. Gather the lower edge of the lace tightly and sew around the point as before.

3 Select the most attractive floral and geometric motifs from the lace fragments. Cut them out carefully, close to the edge, and arrange them, taking time to find the best design.

4 Sew the appliqué shapes in place with stab or slip stitches, making sure that the stitchery on the back of the handkerchief is as neat as possible. Make three corners the same and the fourth more elaborate, or add embroidered dates and initials as you wish.

Beaded Hat Pin

There is no better excuse than a wedding for female friends and family members to splurge on a new hat. What better way to embellish it for a special day than with this charming hat pin, which recalls the elegance of times past?

CHOOSING YOUR MATERIALS

This hat pin is deceptively easy to create, and would be a perfect way for the bride to express her thanks to the close friends who have given their time to help with organizing and arranging the festivities. The trellis-like heart is made from small glass beads threaded onto gold jewelry wire, which is soft and pliable. Use round-nosed pliers to manipulate and tighten the wire. The heart is attached to a basic hat-pin shaft, which can be bought from craft suppliers.

YOU WILL NEED:

Hat pin shaft with safety cover for the point
★
1yd (1m) of 0.6 gauge gold jewelry wire
★
Small round glass beads
★
Round-nosed jewelry pliers
★
Wire cutters
★
PROJECT TIME *2 hours*

1 Cut a 1yd (90cm) length of wire. Bend it in half and make a small loop at the midway point. Slip this onto the pin shaft and slide the loop up to around 1in (2.5cm) from the top. Holding one end of the wire taut, wrap the other end tightly in a spiral around it for a distance of ⅓in (8mm).

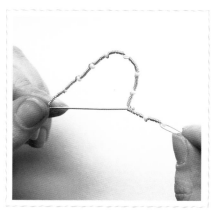

2 Thread a bead onto the taut core wire, and passing the other wire over the bead, continue to wrap for another ⅓in (8mm). Repeat until the wrapped wire measures 3½in (9cm). Following the design given in the Templates section, bend the wire to form one half of the outer heart shape. Secure to the top of the pin shaft by looping the core wire around the shaft. Wrap and bead another 3½in (9cm) of wire in the same way.

42

3 Bend the second half of the heart into shape, and loop the core wire around the pin. Complete the heart by wrapping both ends of the wire around the pin shaft. Continue winding both ends around the central shaft for ½in (15mm), working upward toward the center of the heart.

4 Fill in one side of the heart by wrapping and beading a further 1½in (4cm) of wire and securing it to the top of the outer heart, as shown. Wrap and bead another 1¼in (3cm), bring the ends of the wire back to the shaft, and repeat for the other side.

5 When the heart is complete, wrap both wires up to the top of the pin and trim with wire cutters. Make sure that no sharp ends protrude by turning them under with round-nosed pliers.

43

Beaded Hat Pin

To make a matching brooch, build up the heart shape around a plain length of wire instead of a pin shaft, and mount it onto a jewelry backing.

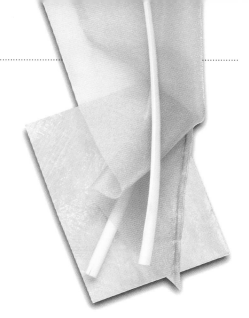

Hat Trick

You do not have to be a milliner to create a stunning hat for a formal occasion. With a little bit of flair and a few well-chosen trimmings, a simple straw base can be turned into a head-turning new creation.

CHOOSING YOUR MATERIALS

44

You may already have a hat that is in need of a new look, or you may prefer to buy a basic shape to remodel. When choosing a hat, always bear in mind the outfit you will be wearing with it, and look for shapes and colors that will both complement your clothing and flatter your face. Remember that wide brims can overwhelm delicate features, while small hats may look out of place on a taller figure. Department stores usually carry a selection of fabric flowers, but it is worth hunting out specialty stores that offer more variety. The quills should be added at the last moment, so that the hat can be transported easily in a hat box.

A white or cream version of this hat would be ideal for a bride who does not wish to wear a traditional dress and veil for her wedding.

YOU WILL NEED:

Straw hat
★
1yd (90cm) of silk organza
★
2 silk flowers
★
2 quills or long feathers
★
Matching sewing thread
★
Basic sewing kit
★
PROJECT TIME *4 hours*

1 Remove any existing trimmings from the hat, making sure that you do not snip into the straw. Keep any trimmings that you do remove, as you may find that they can be used for another project. Carefully clean off any dust with a soft cloth.

2 Cut two bias strips from the organza, 5½in (14cm) and 15in (38cm) wide. These should be cut across the whole width of the fabric. Fold the narrow piece in half lengthwise and pin the two long edges together to form the binding. Turn in the edge at one short end by ½in (15mm) to neaten.

Hat Trick

3 Starting at the center back of the hat, pin the raw edges of the binding to the outside edge of the brim. Start with the unneatened end of the binding. Match the edges carefully, and place the pins ½in (15mm) from the edge of the brim.

4 Wrap the loose, neatened end of the binding strip over the other end to make a neat join. Sew the binding in place through the straw with large, loose stitches, then gently ease the folded edge down and over the edge of the brim. Do not pull it taut.

5 Loosely slip stitch the folded edge to the underside of the brim, passing the needle under a few threads of fabric, then through two strands of straw.

6 Fold under ½in (15mm) along each long edge of the wide organza strip, and gather it loosely at one end. Stitch the folds together, then pin this end just to the right of the center back on the crown of the hat. Secure with a few loose stitches. Holding the hat steady in one hand, drape the fabric around the crown with the other.

Hat Trick

7 Drape the fabric all around the crown, stopping to the left of the center back, so that the first end of the organza strip is covered. Arrange the folds at the loose end into a series of attractive pleats. These do not have to be perfectly symmetrical. Baste the folds together and trim the surplus fabric.

8 Tuck the trimmed end under the folded band, being careful not to pull it out of shape, and secure with a few loose stitches.

9 Keep the band of fabric securely in place by sewing it down at regular intervals with stab stitch. Sew between the folds and keep the stitches very small, so that no thread is visible.

10 Hold the two silk roses so that the flowers lie in opposite directions, facing outward. Sew them firmly together at the center, passing the needle through the stems if possible, or bind them with sewing thread.

11 Pin the flowers at the front of the band. Check that they are in the right position by trying on the hat and looking in a mirror. Adjust as necessary, then stab stitch them in place through all the layers.

12 As the finishing touch, tuck the two quills under the band, so that they sweep backward, and secure with a few stitches. If they are being added at the last minute, use masking tape to hold them in place.

An extravagant hat for a summer
wedding could be decorated with a
band of flowers attached around the
crown to create a garland effect. For
a winter event, choose a felt hat to
match your outfit, and drape it with
a band of patterned silk.

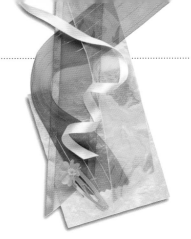

Posy Hair Decoration

This flower-covered barrette is the ideal hair accessory for guests at a less formal wedding, or for those who prefer to put their hair up rather than wearing a hat. It would look equally attractive if worn by an older bridesmaid or matron of honor.

CHOOSING YOUR MATERIALS

The sheer ribbon roses that decorate this barrette are made from printed organza ribbon instead of the more usual satin or taffeta. This is available in assorted colors and several widths, and so can easily be matched to a suit or dress fabric. A large oval padded barrette is used as the foundation, and the roses are attached with a glue gun. If you cannot find a ready-made barrette of the right size, cut a piece of cardboard to size, cover it with batting and satin, and glue a clasp to the wrong side.

48

YOU WILL NEED:

4yds (350cm) of 1½in (4cm) wide sheer floral ribbon
★
1yd (90cm) of 1½in (4cm) wide sheer terra cotta ribbon
★
2yds (180cm) of 1½in (4cm) wide sheer gold-edged spruce ribbon
★
3yds (270cm) of ⅜in (1cm) wide pale green satin ribbon
★
5in (13cm) oval barrette
★
Matching sewing thread
★
Glue gun
★
Basic sewing kit
★
PROJECT TIME *4 hours*

2 Fold the horizontal strip of ribbon to the back at a right angle, about ½in (15mm) along from the coiled center. Pin the fold and turn the rose center until the strip of ribbon is horizontal again. Sew down at the base. Repeat this process, building up the petals, until all the ribbon is coiled.

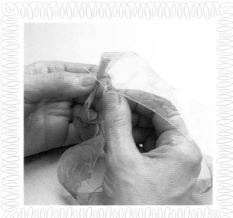

1 Cut a 20in (50cm) length of floral ribbon for each rose. Fold one end forward at a right angle so that it extends below the horizontal section of the ribbon by ½in (15mm). Coil the folded part of the ribbon six times to form a tight tube, and secure at the base with a few over stitches. Keep the thread hanging loose as you make the rose. The stitching point will be slightly higher for each petal.

3 Pleat the raw edge around the base of the rose and wrap the thread around it to form a short stem. Sew in the end and trim close to the thread.

4 To make the leaves, cut fourteen 4in (10cm) lengths of spruce ribbon. Fold the ends down the center to form a triangle. Pin and secure at the lower edge with a few stitches. Fold the outside edges in toward the middle and stitch, then repeat this once more to form a leaf shape. Wrap the thread around the base, and tie off.

5 Cut the pale green and terra cotta ribbon into 3in (8cm) lengths. Fold each in half widthwise and gather the bottom edge. Wrap the thread around to make a stem, and stitch securely.

6 Using a glue gun, glue ten of the leaves in clusters around the edges of the barrette, so that half of each leaf overhangs the edge. Arrange the roses over the center of the barrette and glue in position. Glue the remaining leaves between the roses.

Posy Hair Decoration

7 Glue the terra cotta loops between the roses to cover the background fabric and fill in any gaps at the edges of the barrette. Glue the pale green loops randomly between the loops, leaves, and roses. Cut the remaining satin ribbon into 12in (30cm) lengths and glue to the back of the barrette.

Beautiful Doll

Being chosen as a flower girl is an exciting event for a young girl, and one that she will always remember. This adorable doll, dressed in a miniature version of the little girl's own silk dress, is more than just a toy and will be cherished for years to come.

CHOOSING YOUR MATERIALS

The doll's body is made from knitted stockinette fabric and stuffed with polyfil stuffing, which gives her the typically cuddly appearance that all the best rag dolls should have. If you wish, the basic dress pattern can be altered for a higher waistline or shorter sleeves, so that it more closely matches the flower girl's dress. To personalize the doll, make the hair and sew the eyes with embroidery thread that reflects the child's individual coloring. With a little thought, the finished doll will have a real character of her own and be a friend for life!

1 Make a paper pattern for each piece, as shown in the Templates section. Cut the body parts from stockinette. Stitch the head darts, then join the short edges. Turn ½in (15mm) along the neck edge to the wrong side and baste. Stitch the body pieces together, leaving the neck open. Sew the arms in pairs, leaving the top open. Snip between fingers and thumb and notch the curves. Stitch the sides of the legs together, then sew on the soles of the feet. Turn all parts right side out.

2 Stuff the legs firmly, match the front and back seams, and oversew the top. Stuff the arms to 1½in (4cm) below the top, and oversew the top neatly. Stitch three finger lines on each hand. Stuff the body, working the filling into the corners and up to the neck.

To complete the doll's wardrobe, the dress pattern could be made up in white cotton to make an old-fashioned nightdress.

3 Fit the lower edge of the head over the neck with the seam to center back. Sew in place with tiny stitches. Stuff the head firmly, molding and shaping as you go. Run a gathering thread around the top, 1in (2.5cm) below the edge, draw up tightly, and tie off. Trim the excess fabric.

4 Pin the arms in place over the shoulders, so they hang naturally down the side with thumbs facing forward. Oversew securely, and oversew the legs to the lower edge of the body.

5 Cut the "hair" into 16in (40cm) lengths and backstitch to the tape at their mid-points, making a center parting to fit from the forehead to the nape of the neck. Fold under the ends of the tape, then pin to the head and backstitch in place along the parting. Twist several loops of thread to make a fringe and glue above the hairline, then glue down the hair on either side of the parting. Divide the hair into ten bunches. Twist each one into a ringlet, trim as necessary, tuck the ends under the hair, and stitch to the head at the neck edge.

6 Draw in the features lightly with pencil. The eyes are composed of two circles of buttonhole stitch, with a black pupil and blue iris. They are outlined in black stem stitch with straight stitch eyelashes. Highlight each pupil with a white French knot and indicate the nose with two black French knots. Stitch the lips in satin stitch, and color the cheeks with a blusher pencil.

Beautiful Doll

7 Cut two pantaloon pieces from cotton lawn. Stitch the leg seams, then hand roll and hem the raw edges of the crotch seams. Turn a ¼in (6mm) casing at the top of each leg. Hem the bottom of the legs and trim with lace. Thread narrow ribbon through the casing, slip the pantaloons onto the doll's legs, and tie the ribbon at the front.

8 Cut a 6 x 25in (15 x 60cm) rectangle of cotton lawn for the petticoat. Sew the back seam, leaving the top 1½in (4cm) unstitched. Hand roll and hem the opening. Hem the bottom edge and trim with lace. Cut a 1in (2.5cm) strip for the waistband and gather the top edge of the petticoat to fit. Pin, baste, and sew the band to the gathered edge. Turn in the ends, fold the band over to the inside, and hem in place. Sew on a button and a buttonhole loop to fasten.

9 Cut the dress pieces from silk. Stitch the bodice front to the backs at the shoulders. Stitch a piece of tape across the wrong side of each sleeve to form a casing 1in (2.5cm) up from the straight edge. Thread a 4in (10cm) length of narrow pink ribbon through each side of the casings and through to the front in the middle of the sleeves, securing at the outside edges. Hem the cuffs and trim with lace. Gather the tops of the sleeves, then pin and stitch them to the bodice. Stitch the sleeve and side seams in one continuous line.

10 Stitch the skirt seams, leaving the top 1½in (4cm) open at the back. Gather the top edge, then pin, baste, and machine stitch to the bodice, distributing the folds evenly. Hand roll and neaten the neck edge and hemline. Sew the buttons along one side of the opening, and make corresponding loops on the other side. Cut a 24in (61cm) length of floral ribbon and sew invisibly to the front of the bodice along the bottom edge.

11 Cut two of each bonnet piece from interfacing and iron on the silk. Cut around each shape, leaving ¼in (6mm) of silk all around. With right sides together, stitch the front edges of the brims. Trim, notch, and turn right side out. Baste the raw edges together. Stitch each bonnet back to a crown. Stitch the brim to the front of one crown piece along the basting line. Gather a piece of floral ribbon to fit inside the brim along the seam line. Turn over the raw edges around the rest of the bonnet. Pin and baste the bonnet lining in place and slip stitch all remaining seams. Drape a 20in (50cm) length of ribbon over the bonnet and stitch at the neck edge. Cover the stitches by gluing on a few flowers.

12 Cut the shoes from felt. Sew the back seams, then attach the soles with buttonhole stitch. Fix a small bow to the front of each shoe. Make a tiny posy from silk flowers and tie it with two lengths of ¼in (8mm) pink ribbon. Dress the doll and stitch the posy to one hand.

Victorian Cornucopia

A cornucopia, or horn of plenty, is a pleasing wedding theme. This lace-trimmed symbol of plenty and abundance – based on a Victorian original – makes a charming alternative to the more usual bridesmaid's posy or flower basket.

54

YOU WILL NEED:

6 x 12in (15 x 30cm) of thin cardboard

★

8 x 14in (17 x 32cm) of silk or satin

★

Pencil and ruler

★

Pair of compasses and protractor

★

12in (30cm) of 1½in (4cm) wide lace edging

★

4in (10cm) square block of florist's foam

★

Kitchen knife

★

Craft glue

★

Double-sided adhesive tape

★

6 sprays of silk flowers

★

Wire cutters

★

1 spray of silk ivy leaves

★

Reel of fine wire for binding

★

1yd (90cm) each of ⅓in (8mm) wide picot-edged ribbon in three colors

★

24in (60cm) of ⅓in (8mm) wide picot-edged ribbon for handle

★

2 large pins

★

PROJECT TIME 3 *hours*

CHOOSING YOUR MATERIALS

In past times, the bride and groom's path from the church was strewn with flowers to bring good luck and prosperity. The bouquets and floral arrangements carried by today's attendants are a reminder of this custom. This silk-flower filled cornucopia is easy to carry and has the advantage that it will last for many years. The basic cone shape can be made to match or contrast with the bridesmaids' dresses, and the selection of flowers and leaves repeated for a coordinating garland headdress.

1 Draw a 6in (15cm) diameter semicircle onto cardboard, and cut out. Measure a 20-degree angle at the center and draw a line at this angle to the outside edge. Cut along this line, then snip out a small v-shape at the center point. Coat the card lightly with glue and stick it to the wrong side of the fabric. Trim the surplus fabric, leaving a ¾in (2cm) margin. Snip into this allowance and neaten the edges by folding them over and gluing them to the cardboard.

2 Attach a length of double-sided adhesive tape to one edge of the covered card, on the right side. Peel off the backing paper and bend the card carefully. Press the two edges together to form a cone.

3 Placing the overlapped ends so that they line up with the join, fix the top edge of the lace to the inside of the cone with double-sided tape to form a border.

4 Trim the florist's foam into a rough ball shape with a kitchen knife, remembering to cut away from you at all times. Check that it will fit inside the cone, then glue the ball into place.

5 Cut six sprays of ivy, and sticking the stems into the foam, arrange them around the rim of the cone at evenly spaced intervals. Cut the silk flowers into single sprays and fix into the foam. Start in the center and work outward, so that the colors are evenly distributed. Make sure no foam is visible between the stems.

Victorian Cornucopia

6 Cut the three long ribbons into 12in (30cm) lengths. Taking two pieces at a time, fold them into loops with overlapping tails and secure at the center with wire. Fix around the outside edge of the arrangement. Tie a bow at each end of the remaining ribbon and glue to either side of the rim to make a carrying handle. Push a large pin through the cone and into the foam to make it doubly secure.

Cinderella Slippers

Every little girl would love to wear a beautiful gown and star in her own fairy story, so make the youngest bridesmaid's dream come true with a pair of satin slippers worthy of a princess.

56

Choosing your Materials

A pair of ordinary satin ballet pumps can be glamorized by adding long ribbon ties and a trimming of lace, ribbon roses, and realistic silk ivy leaves. The basic shoes are usually available in white or the dancer's favorite shade of soft peach, but can be dyed to match the color of the dress fabric. A band of narrow elastic sewn across the instep will help to keep the slippers in place on tiny feet. Plain satin shoes for older bridesmaids can be decorated in the same way, omitting the ties.

You will need:

THE AMOUNTS GIVEN ARE FOR SHOES TO FIT A TODDLER – SCALE UP THE MEASUREMENTS FOR A LARGER SIZE

Satin ballet shoes
★
24in (60cm) of ⅛in (3mm) wide white ribbon
★
20in (50cm) of ⅓in (8mm) wide lace edging
★
2yds (180cm) of ⅓in (8mm) wide ribbon with a decorative edge for ties
★
2 large and 8 small ribbon roses
★
10 small silk leaves
★
Matching sewing thread
★
Basic sewing kit
★
PROJECT TIME *1 hour*

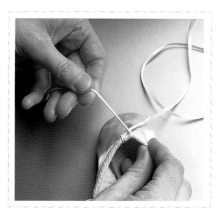

1 Cut the narrow ribbon in two. Undo the bow at the front of the shoe and sew one end of the ribbon to the cord. Pull the other end of the cord gently until the sewn end of the ribbon appears, then cut off. Do the same with the other shoe.

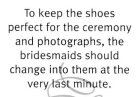

To keep the shoes perfect for the ceremony and photographs, the bridesmaids should change into them at the very last minute.

2 Cut the lace edging in half and make a narrow hem at both ends. Sew one length around the top of each shoe, starting and finishing either side of the tie. Be careful not to stick the needle into the channel or the ribbon will get caught up in the stitches.

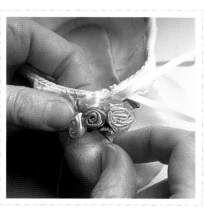

3 Sew a large ribbon rose to the center front of the shoe, close to the tie, then stitch two smaller roses on either side. Do the same on the other shoe, making sure they match exactly.

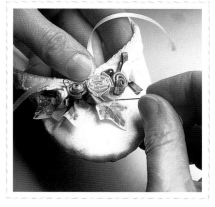

4 Sew on the ivy leaves so that they lie in the spaces between the silk flowers.

5 Cut the ribbon for the ties into four equal lengths, and neaten both ends of each. Sew one ribbon securely to either side of each shoe, lining them up with the inside seams. Make sure that the stitches are concealed by the lace trim.

Cinderella Slippers

Circlet of Flowers

A floral garland makes a simple yet stunning headdress for a bridesmaid of any age. This enchanting symbol of spring will flatter everyone, from the matron of honor to the smallest flower girl.

CHOOSING YOUR MATERIALS

The circlet is made from realistic fabric blooms, so it will not wilt or become damaged. There are now almost as many different types of silk flowers available as there are varieties of fresh blooms, and you will find a wide selection at many department stores, florists, or garden centers. When making your choice, look out especially for sprays of smaller blossoms that will divide easily into small bunches, rather than larger single flowers. Work to a color scheme of two or three main shades to coordinate with the bridesmaids' dresses, then add in a few sprays of trailing variegated ivy leaves and matching gauzy bows and streamers.

A hoop of fresh or silk flowers, made in the same way but on a larger scale, makes an unusual alternative to a bouquet for the youngest bridesmaids to carry.

58

YOU WILL NEED:

14in (36cm) lengths of medium wire for circlet and stems
★
Green floral (gutta percha) tape
★
Small pliers
★
8 sprays of silk flowers
★
2 sprays of silk ivy leaves
★
1½yds (140cm) each of 2in (5cm) wide organdy ribbon in two toning colors
★
PROJECT TIME *3 hours*

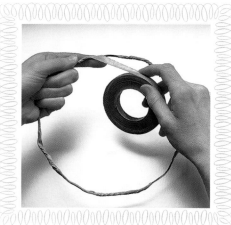

1 Measure the circumference of the wearer's head and add on 2in (5cm). Twist several pieces of wire together until they equal this length, then bend into a circle. Secure the ends with pliers, making sure that no wires protrude. Cover with several rounds of floral tape, adding extra layers over the joins.

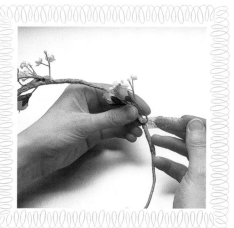

2 Cut the silk flowers into individual sprays. To make sure that the various colors are evenly spaced, divide the hoop into four sections, and fix the first flowers at the quarter marks. Hold each spray close to the foundation wire, and bind tape around the stem.

3 Continue covering the hoop in this way until the foundation is completely concealed, making sure the flowers all lie in the same direction. Add ivy sprays and leaves as you go, and alternate the shapes and colors of the flowers.

4 Cut three 8in (20cm) lengths from both ribbons. Fold each piece into a flat loop, overlapping the ends for ¾in (2cm) at the back. Bend over the top 1in (2.5cm) of a short length of wire, and hook this over the center of the loop. Twist with pliers to hold the bow securely and form a stem. Attach the bows to the hoop at regular intervals, covering any wire ends with tape.

5 When the garland is complete, fold the remaining ribbons in half and wire them together. Fix to the back of the garland to form streamers, then trim the ends at an angle. The garland should sit comfortably on the wearer's head, but for extra security, can be held in place with hair pins.

Circlet of Flowers

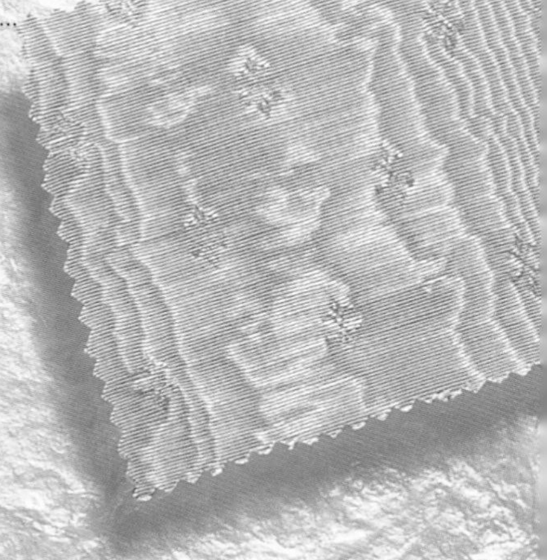

Ring Bearer Style

Little boys love dressing up just as much as little girls. This bow tie and cummerbund set is a scaled-down version of adult formal wear, which will make even the most mischievous and unruly little boy look ready for the occasion.

CHOOSING YOUR MATERIALS

The ring bearer's outfit can be coordinated with the ties, cravats, and vests worn by the groom, best man, and ushers, or may pick up the shade of the bridesmaids' dresses. Plain colors, or smaller patterns and repeats work best for children's clothes, including paisleys, tartans, and stripes. Search furnishing as well as dressmaking suppliers for unusual materials and remnants; the pearl grey moiré taffeta used here is, in fact, a curtain fabric. You could use the remnants to cover a set of small buttons to sew onto a white shirt in place of adult cufflinks and shirt studs.

YOU WILL NEED:

24in (50cm) wide rectangle of fabric; the length should be the waist measurement plus 2in (5cm)

★

4 hook and eye sets

★

Matching sewing thread

★

Sewing machine

★

Basic sewing kit

★

PROJECT TIME *3 hours*

1 Cut out a rectangle measuring 5½ x 9in (14 x 23cm) for the tie. With right sides together, sew the two short ends together, ½in (15mm) from the edge. Leave a 1½in (4cm) gap in the center of the stitch line. Press the seam open. Fold so that the seam lies along the center back, then stitch the two sides together.

2 Clip the corners and turn right side out. Ease into shape and press. Sew two parallel lines of large running stitch down the center, and draw up the thread.

3 Oversew the outside edges of the center on the reverse side, to form the bow. Cut a 2 x 1½in (5 x 4cm) strip of fabric and press under ½in (15mm) along each long and one short side. Wrap this around the center of the bow, with the neatened short end overlapping the other short end, and stitch in place at the back.

4 Cut a 2in (5cm) wide strip to fit the collar measurement, adding an extra 2in (5cm) to the length for turnings. Fold in half lengthwise, with right sides together, and stitch the long sides together ¼in (6mm) from the edge. Turn the tube right side out and press so that the seam lies at the center back. Sew the bow to the center, then neaten the raw ends. Check the fit, then sew on a hook and eye to fasten.

5 For the cummerbund, cut a 10in (25cm) wide strip of fabric the same length as the waist measurement, plus 2in (5cm) for turnings. Press under 1in (2.5cm) along each long edge, then press into a series of three 1in (2.5cm) pleats. Sew the pleats in place, stitching under the folds so that the thread does not show.

6 To line, cut a rectangle the same size as the finished cummerbund. Press under ⅜in (1cm) along each long edge, then pin and slip stitch to the back. Fold under a double ⅜in (1cm) hem at either short end and press. Sew on three hook and eye sets to fasten.

Bear Essentials

No teddy should be without a trendy vest for public events! This dandyish brocade version can be made for a much-loved companion who will be attending the wedding with his small owner, or for a new bear to be given as a gift to a ring bearer or flower girl.

CHOOSING YOUR MATERIALS

The vest is made from striped woven brocade and lined with textured silk tussore. All bears vary in size and shape, so you will have to adjust the basic pattern to obtain the correct fitting. Before cutting into the main fabric, cut the pieces from calico, like a couturier making a toile (a pattern made up in cheap cloth as a test). Baste them together, then alter the armholes and shoulder seams as necessary, so that they will fit your bear comfortably. The ensemble is completed with a tiny version of the ring bearer's bow tie (see page 60) made from taffeta ribbon and sewn onto a length of elastic.

62

The dress pattern for the rag doll could be enlarged and adapted as an alternative outfit for a "girl" bear.

YOU WILL NEED:

THE AMOUNTS OF FABRIC REQUIRED WILL VARY DEPENDING ON SIZE OF BEAR

Paper and pencil
★
Brocade for outside of vest
★
Silk for vest lining
★
2 gold buttons
★
Matching sewing thread
★
Sewing machine
★
Basic sewing kit
★
PROJECT TIME *3 hours*

1 Trace the front and back pattern pieces from the Templates section, and adjust them to fit your bear. Cut out two fronts and one back from lining and brocade, making sure that any stripes or checks match.

2 With right sides together, sew the main fabric pieces together at the sides and shoulders, leaving a ⅜in (1cm) seam allowance. Make up the lining in the same way. Press the seams open.

5 Pin, then baste and slip stitch the two layers together around the armholes. Press the vest carefully, using a pressing cloth to protect the fabric.

4 Clip the seam allowance around the armholes, and baste to the wrong side on both the lining and the brocade.

3 Place the two pieces right sides together and pin around the outside edge, matching the joins carefully. Baste, then stitch along the seam line, leaving a 1½in (4cm) gap at the lower edge of the center back. Clip the corners and notch the curves. Turn right side out and slip stitch the gap closed.

6 Sew two decorative buttons to the right front. It is not necessary to make buttonholes.

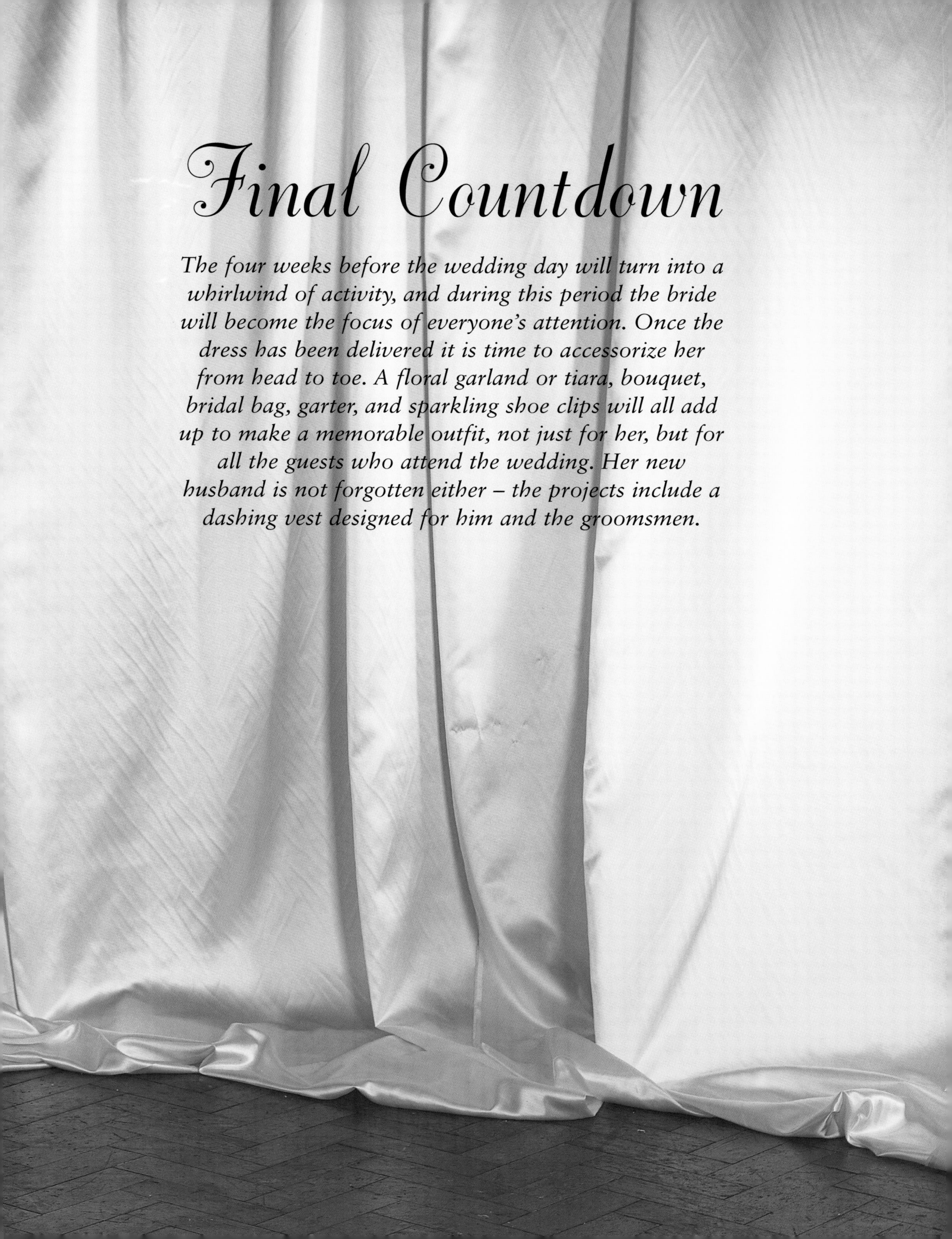

Final Countdown

The four weeks before the wedding day will turn into a whirlwind of activity, and during this period the bride will become the focus of everyone's attention. Once the dress has been delivered it is time to accessorize her from head to toe. A floral garland or tiara, bouquet, bridal bag, garter, and sparkling shoe clips will all add up to make a memorable outfit, not just for her, but for all the guests who attend the wedding. Her new husband is not forgotten either – the projects include a dashing vest designed for him and the groomsmen.

For the Groom

Inevitably the fashion focus of a wedding falls on the bride, but the groom should not be left out of the fun. Although his formal wear may be rented just for the day, why not make him a stylish vest that will both complement the jacket and express his personality?

CHOOSING YOUR MATERIALS

Experienced dressmakers may wish to start from scratch and make a tailored vest from a paper pattern, but if you want to save time, simply revamp a ready-made garment as shown here. Choose an open-backed design for a summer wedding or if the groom is not going to take off his jacket after the service. Good needlecraft stores will stock an assortment of items that can be used as trimmings; look for cords, ready-made pipings, Chinese knotted buttons, and the military-style toggle fastenings known as "frogs."

66

YOU WILL NEED:

Black frog fastenings –
one for each existing button

★

Cord piping to fit around front
edges of vest

★

Matching and contrasting
sewing thread

★

Basic sewing kit

★

PROJECT TIME *3 hours*

1 Snip off the buttons, being careful not to cut into the fabric. Remove any traces of thread, and mark the position of each button with a pin.

For a stunning ensemble effect, the best man and the ushers could all be dressed in matching vests, in the same or complementary fabrics.

2 Slip stitch the buttonholes together on the reverse side of the vest, using sewing thread that matches the lining fabric to produce an invisible join.

3 Turn under one end of the piping, and attach it to the lower front side seam. Pin the piping around the lower and opening edges of the vest front, and across the back of the neck. Ease it gently to fit around the curves and corners, and take it all the way around to the other front side seam. Neaten the end, and slip stitch in place with matching sewing thread.

4 Keep the flat edge of the piping in place by sewing it loosely to the lining with herringbone stitch in a contrasting color.

5 Lay the vest flat on your work surface and line up the front edges so that any pattern matches across the two sides. Pin the frog fastenings across the opening.

6 Sew the fastenings in place with stab stitch, using a thimble to protect your finger. Because the frogs are handmade, no two will be exactly alike, so do not worry if they are not quite symmetrical.

Romantic Ring Pillow

The continuous knot design appliquéed to this lace-edged ring pillow is a time-honored symbol of never-ending love, which has been used to decorate love tokens from Valentines to wedding quilts for very many years.

CHOOSING YOUR MATERIALS

The pillow cover itself is made from damask, and the texture of the cotton contrasts well with the smooth satin knot and the lavish lace frill. Choose rich cream or crisp white fabrics and lace, depending on the color of the bride's dress. The small bunches of silk flowers that decorate the corners should match those in her bouquet. Instead of making a special pillow form, you could fill the pillow with batting and scent it with a handful of potpourri or dried rose petals.

68

YOU WILL NEED:

6in (15cm) square of fusible web

★

6in (15cm) square of cream satin

★

9 x 16in (23 x 40cm) of pale cream damask

★

30in (75cm) of ³⁄₄in (2cm) wide lace edging

★

24 x 33in (60 x 85cm) of batting

★

2yds (180cm) of 3in (8cm) wide double-edged lace

★

Selection of small silk flowers

★

12in (30cm) of ⅛in (3mm) wide cream ribbon

★

Matching sewing thread

★

Sewing machine

★

Basic sewing kit

★

PROJECT TIME *4 hours*

1 Draw the knot motif from the Templates section onto fusible web and iron it to the wrong side of the satin. Cut out carefully along the pencil outline. Cut the damask into two 8 x 9in (20 x 23cm) rectangles. Remove the backing paper from the fusible web, and iron the knot centrally onto one of the pieces of damask.

2 Thread the sewing machine with matching thread and set to a narrow satin stitch. Sew over the edges of the motif, following the interlacing lines on the template.

3 Cut a length of the narrow lace to fit along each side of the pillow front, and pin in place ³⁄₄in (2cm) from the edge with the scallops facing inward. Stitch down. With right sides facing, sew the back and front of the pillow together along three sides.

4 To make the pillow form, cut twelve pieces of batting: four 8 x 9in (30 x 23cm), four 7 x 8in (18 x 20cm), and four 6 x 7in (15 x 18cm). Sandwich together, with the smallest pieces on the inside, then sew around the outside edges. Insert the form into the pillow cover and slip stitch the fourth side together.

5 Sew the two ends of the wide lace together to form a loop, fold into four, and mark the quarters with pins. Sew four gathering threads around the lace between the pins, about ¼in (6mm) in from the edge. Pin the quarter marks to the corners of the pillow and draw up the gathers. Pin and stitch the lace along the seam lines.

6 Pin, then hand stitch two or three small silk flowers securely to each corner of the pillow.

7 Fold the narrow ribbon in half and sew to the center of the satin knot. This will be used to tie the rings to the pillow before the wedding ceremony. A loop of tape can be attached to the back of the pillow to make it easier for the ring bearer to carry.

Jeweled Shoe Clips

When a bride slips her feet into her delicate bridal slippers she will feel that they are the most important pair of shoes that she will ever wear. Whether of the finest leather, brocade, satin, or velvet, they can only be enhanced by the addition of these lily-shaped beaded clips.

CHOOSING YOUR MATERIALS

Shoe clips are a versatile way to personalize the bride's shoes, and the materials used can be adapted to suit her outfit. Choose beads that will tone in with the design details of the bridal dress, or which pick up the theme of the jewelry that she will be wearing – pearl, crystal, or metallic. The beading technique used to make the flowers is very straightforward and easy to learn, even if you are unused to working with wire. You may find it so fascinating that you are inspired to make matching earrings, a necklace, or even a tiara!

70

YOU WILL NEED:

2⅓yds (2m) of 0.6 gauge gold jewelry wire
★
Small translucent and pale blue round glass beads
★
Round-nosed jewelry pliers
★
Wire cutters
★
Shoe clip mounts
★
PROJECT TIME *2 hours*

1 Cut a 20in (50cm) length of wire. Make a small loop ⅓in (8mm) in diameter, 4in (10cm) from one end. Twist into shape with the pliers. This will form the center of the flower.

2 Make the first petal by threading 40 beads onto the long end of the wire, and bending it into a loop. Use clear beads interspersed with a few blue ones to act as highlights. Pass the working wire through and around the flower center to secure.

3 Fill the petal outline by threading 15 beads onto the wire and wrapping it around the top of the loop. Pick up 15 more beads and secure the wire to the flower center, as before.

4 Make the other four petals in the same way. Complete the flower by threading 40 blue beads, and bending them into a flat spiral shape. Push the end of the working wire back through the center of the flower.

5 Fix the flower to the clip by wrapping the two ends of the wire around the upper half of the mount, using pliers to hold them tightly in place. Trim the loose ends with wire clippers, and make sure that no sharp ends protrude by turning them under with the pliers.

An ancient good-luck custom involves throwing an old shoe after the newly married couple. Even today, a pair of old shoes or boots is sometimes tied onto the back of their car as they depart for a new life together.

Good Luck Garter

Tempting as it may be to keep this alluring lace, bead, and sequin ornamented garter, tradition dictates that the bride must remove it after the ceremony and throw it to the assembled guests!

72

You will need:

26in (65cm) of 2½in (6cm) wide lace
★
26in (65cm) of 1½in (4cm) wide lace
★
Small silver and translucent round glass beads
★
Translucent cup sequins
★
Silver star-shaped sequins
★
Size 11 needle
★
26 x 2in (65 x 5cm) of cream satin
★
20in (50cm) of ¼in (6mm) wide elastic
★
20in (50cm) each of ⅓in (8mm) wide picot-edged ribbon in cream and pale blue
★
Small crystal heart or other lucky charm
★
Matching sewing thread
★
Safety pin
★
Sewing machine
★
Basic sewing kit
★
Project time *4 hours*

Choosing your Materials

The garter is an indispensable element of bridal apparel, which has a history deeply rooted in the past. The groom's men once fought among themselves for the ribbons that held up the bride's stockings as soon as the religious service was over. Making the garter is a work of devotion, for it takes care and time to achieve the result you wish for. Look in your work basket for bits of antique lace that will add immeasurably to the effect, and ask family and friends to share in the experience by giving lacy fragments and pretty beads.

A pair of fine silk stockings and a new set of lacy lingerie make the perfect accompaniment for the garter.

1 Decorate the wider length of lace with beads and sequins. Sew a border of cup sequins along the scalloped edge, with a row of silver beads inside. Pick out features such as flower centers and emphasize them with star sequins and translucent beads.

2 With right sides facing, pin and stitch the second length of lace to the first, ½in (15mm) from the straight edge. Trim, then press the seam toward the beaded edge.

3 Fold the satin strip in half lengthwise, and stitch along the length using a ½in (15mm) seam allowance. Turn right sides out by fastening a safety pin to one end and pushing it back through the tube. Press flat so that the seam lies to the back. Pin over the seam on the lace, then stitch in place to form a gathering channel.

4 Trim the two ends of the lace so that they are straight, then with wrong sides together, join the ends of the lace to form a loop. Trim the seam to ⅛in (3mm), open out, and press. Fold the lace right sides together and press the seam flat. Stitch a second seam, enclosing the raw edges, then press the seam to one side. Fasten the safety pin to one end of the elastic, and thread through the channel. Stitch the two ends together.

5 Make a rosette to cover the join by looping the two lengths of ribbon four times. Let the ends hang down as streamers, and secure through the center with stab stitch. Sew onto the garter, and add a small heart or other charm for luck.

Elegant Tiara

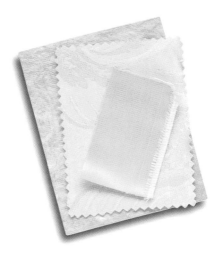

This classic nineteenth-century style headdress will add a sophisticated finishing touch to the wedding outfit and set any hairstyle off to perfection. It would be particularly suitable for a winter wedding, when the bride may be wearing a gown of satin, brocade, or velvet.

CHOOSING YOUR MATERIALS

The tiara is made from machine-embroidered fabric that has been padded with a layer of batting and mounted onto a narrow semi-circular headband. You could use a remnant of the wedding dress if it is patterned, or choose a woven brocade in colors to match. Look for a design that can be highlighted with lines of satin stitch in rich gold thread, to give the distinctive quilted appearance. Take some time to practice this technique on a piece of spare fabric, until you feel confident about free-stitching.

74

YOU WILL NEED:

8 x 14in (20 x 35cm)
of brocade
★
8 x 14in (20 x 35cm) of
heavyweight sew-in interfacing
★
Gold machine embroidery thread
★
8 x 14in (20 x 35cm) of satin
for lining
★
8 x 14in (20 x 35cm) of batting
★
Matching sewing thread
★
32in (80cm) of narrow lace edging
★
Narrow gold headband
★
Contrasting basting thread
★
Clothespin
★
Sewing machine
★
Basic sewing kit
★
PROJECT TIME *2 hours*

3 Unpick the basting thread, then baste the batting and the satin lining to the wrong side of the embroidered brocade.

1 Following the design given in the Templates section, cut out the basic tiara pattern from paper, then cut one shape each in brocade, interfacing, batting, and satin. Baste the interfacing to the wrong side of the brocade.

2 Thread the machine with gold thread. Set the controls to a medium-width zigzag and drop the feed dog (the instruction manual will show you how to do this). Starting from the center and working out to each side in turn, stitch slowly and carefully around the woven design.

6 Hand stitch the lace in place around the edges of the tiara, using matching thread. Make sure that the scalloped edge of the lace extends beyond the upper edge of the tiara, and that the straight edge of the lace aligns with the hair band along the lower edge.

4 Machine stitch all four layers together around the outside edge, using gold thread and a zigzag stitch. Carefully remove the basting stitches.

5 Match the center lower edge of the tiara to the middle of the hair band and clip the two together with a clothespin. Over stitch the lower edge of the tiara securely to the front side of the band with small, neat stitches.

Crowning Glory

With its lush roses and anemones, this floral band makes an exquisite headdress for a summer bride, especially if her bridesmaids are accessorized with coordinating garlands. Charming on its own, it could also be worn with a gathered veil for a more formal look.

CHOOSING YOUR MATERIALS

The silk flowers are attached to a plain satin hairband, using a hot-glue gun to keep them securely in place. You will need a range of different shapes and sizes in closely toning shades. If you cannot find artificial blooms in the exact colors you require, white or cream flowers can be sprayed with quick-drying craft paint. The large single blooms are softened by interspersing them with small sprays of silk berries and delicate gypsophila, or "baby's breath," a traditional wedding flower.

2 Using craft glue, carefully secure the double-edged lace around the inside of the hairband to conceal the join.

YOU WILL NEED:

3 large, 6 medium, and
6 small silk flowers

★

Spray craft paint (optional)

★

Cream padded satin hairband

★

16in (40cm) of double-edged lace

★

Craft glue

★

Scissors

★

Gold metallic sewing thread

★

1 spray of silk rose leaves

★

1 spray of artificial or dried gypsophila

★

1 spray of artificial berries

★

Glue gun

★

PROJECT TIME *2 hours*

1 If desired, spray the tips of some of the flower petals with a light coat of craft paint in your chosen color, and allow to dry.

3 Cut the gypsophila into small individual sprays and bind them together with sewing thread. Knot the ends securely.

4 Cut the individual rose leaves from the stem. With the glue gun, fix three of them to each end of the hairband. Glue the three largest flowers across the center, then add three medium and three small flowers down each side.

5 Fill the spaces between alternate flowers along the top and bottom of the hairband by gluing on the sprays of gypsophila.

6 Complete the band by adding small sprays of berries in any gaps. Sew a gathered veil to the underside of the hairband if required.

Crowning Glory

Everlasting Bouquet

No bridal ensemble is complete without a bouquet. The joy of this breathtaking arrangement, constructed from a mixture of dried green foliage and silk flowers, along with pretty pearl sprays and jacquard ribbons, is that it can be preserved for years to come.

78

YOU WILL NEED:

Bouquet holder with 3in (7cm) diameter dry foam ball

★

Reindeer moss

★

Asparagus fern

★

1 spray of artificial or dried gypsophila

★

Selection of silk roses and buds (around 30 heads)

★

14in (36cm) lengths of medium wire for stems

★

Reel of fine wire for binding

★

Green floral (gutta percha) tape

★

2yds (180cm) of 1½in (4cm) wide white jacquard ribbon

★

2yds (180cm) of ½in (16mm) wide white jacquard ribbon

★

Pearl sprays

★

Glue gun

★

Scissors

★

Wire cutters

★

Pliers

★

PROJECT TIME *6 hours*

CHOOSING YOUR MATERIALS

To make the bouquet, you may wish to put together a selection of similar flowers in several colors, as shown, or you may prefer to vary the types of flower while keeping them within the same tonal range. The dramatic cascade effect is created by varying the length of the wire stems to which the flowers are attached. Be sure to make up all the flowers before fixing them into the holder, so that you can get an overall picture of how the finished bouquet will appear. The foam, wires, and other materials are available from florists and garden centers.

1 Cut several wire stems into 4in (10cm) lengths, then bend over one end of each to form a hook. Use these to secure pieces of reindeer moss over the foam inside the bouquet holder, so that it is completely concealed.

2 Take several sprays of gypsophila and bind them together with fine wire, then bind the completed spray securely to one end of a wire stem.

3 Cover the wire with florist's tape, spiral binding it tightly. Fix individual roses and their leaves onto wire stems and cover them in the same way. Remember to make sure that they are all different lengths for a natural effect.

4 Cut one long and two shorter stems of asparagus fern. Fix the long piece into the foam so that it will hang downward. Position the other two pieces on either side to form a triangle; this will be the basic shape of the arrangement. Glue the ends of the stems to the foam so they stay firmly in place. Starting with the smallest flowers at the lower edge, fix the roses and buds into the foam.

5 Continue to arrange the flowers, increasing the size as you work upward and gradually shortening the lengths of the stems. Fill the spaces with gypsophila and pearl sprays.

6 Fold the wide ribbon into a double bow and secure with wire. Cut the narrow ribbon in two, then fold each length in half to form streamers. Fix these to the back of the bow with the glue gun, then glue the bow and streamers to the top edge of the bouquet. As a final touch, glue a single flower to the center of the bow.

Bridal Bag

This delightful bag is just the right size to hold the bride's perfume, lipstick, a lace handkerchief, and all the other small but essential items she will need to keep by her side.

YOU WILL NEED:

18 x 36in (45 x 90cm) of cream silk douppioni

★

18in (45cm) square of medium-weight iron-on interfacing

★

10 x 20in (25 x 50cm) of foamboard

★

12yds (11m) of satin and jacquard ribbons, ³⁄₈ and ¹⁄₂in (10 & 15mm) wide, in assorted creams and whites

★

Pencil and ruler

★

1yd (90cm) of narrow piping cord

★

3 skeins of stranded cream embroidery thread

★

Gold sewing thread

★

10in (25cm) square of white satin

★

14in (36cm) lengths of fine and regular wire for stems

★

Wire cutters

★

White floral (gutta percha) tape

★

2 gold shoe cake decorations

★

Contrasting basting thread

★

Matching sewing thread

★

PROJECT TIME 10 *hours*

CHOOSING YOUR MATERIALS

This project combines two popular crafts – ribbon weaving and flower making – and makes a good starting point for newcomers to either technique. The main body of the bag is made from a woven ribbon panel, in closely toned shades of ivory, cream, and oyster, which echo the colors of the bride's gown and her other accessories. The ribbons are in various widths, which adds interest to the texture of the weave. The matching corsage, which complements the bag perfectly, is complete in itself. It could also be adapted as a buttonhole or hat decoration.

If you find that you enjoy the technique of ribbon weaving, try working on a larger scale to make a pillow cover, or even a larger envelope-style bag.

1 Cut a 6 x 16in (15 x 40cm) rectangle of interfacing and lay it adhesive-side-up on the foamboard. Cut eleven 18in (45cm) lengths of assorted ribbons to form the warp (the lengthwise strands of the ribbon weave). Pin them along one end of the interfacing, leaving a small gap between each.

2 Cut the remaining ribbon into 6in (15cm) lengths and use these to form the weft (the crosswise strands of the ribbon weave). Weave them between the long ribbons, over then under alternately, pinning them at each end to secure.

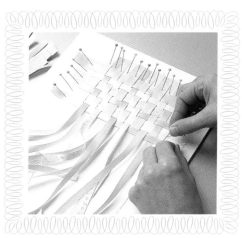

3 Continue to weave, alternating widths, patterns, and colors, until the panel is complete. Cover with a piece of clean, white cloth for protection and press with a hot iron. Remove the pins and press again on the reverse side to attach the interfacing securely.

4 Cut two 1½ x 16in (4 x 40cm) bias strips. Cut the piping cord in half and baste in place inside the strips. With raw edges together, pin and baste the piping to the long edges of the panel. Lay a 12 x 16in (30 x 40cm) rectangle of silk over the panel, matching the top edges. Pin, baste, and sew along the edge of the piping using a zipper foot. Trim the seam allowance to ½in (15mm) and press toward the silk.

5 Fold one short end of the panel over the last two ribbons and pin into a tube, matching the weave carefully. Hand stitch the join invisibly. Machine stitch the rest of the seam, leaving a ½in (15mm) gap 2in (5cm) above the ribbon panel. Press the seam open, and fold the silk to the inside, so that the raw edge covers the top of the ribbon panel. Baste in position.

This project can be
adapted for future use as
an evening bag by
removing the corsage.

82

6 Cut two 5½in (14cm) diameter
circles of silk. Iron one onto
interfacing and trim. With right
sides together, pin and baste along
the piped lower edge. Notch the
seam allowance, and stitch in place.
Turn right sides out. To make the
lining, cut a 5½ x 16in (14 x 40cm)
rectangle of silk. Seam the two
short edges, and sew the second silk
circle to one end. With right sides
inward, fold the top edge to the
wrong side, then fit inside the bag
and stitch in place along the fold.

7 Machine stitch around the bag,
either side of the gap to form a
casing, reinforcing the ends of the
stitch lines. Make two 30in (76cm)
rouleaux (see Techniques &
Templates) and thread through. Tie
the ends together in pairs and trim.
Remove the bands from the
embroidery threads, cut through the
ends, and divide into two equal
bundles. For each tassel, lay the
knot in the middle of a bundle. Lift
the threads around the rouleau, and
tie a thread tightly above the knot.
Pull the threads back down and
wrap gold thread below the knot to
form a neck. Sew in the ends and
trim the tassels neatly.

8 Using the leaf design given in
the Templates section, cut 14
satin leaves and pin in pairs with
right sides together. Stitch around
the outer edge, leaving a small gap
at the base. Notch the curves, and
turn right sides out. Insert a fine
wire down the center of the leaf,
leaving the end protruding.
Machine stitch veins, and then clip
off the excess wire. Attach each leaf
to a piece of regular wire to form a
stem, and wrap with tape to secure.
Make a 10in (25cm) satin rouleau,
and cut into 2in (5cm) lengths.
Thread each rouleau to the center
of a length of regular wire. Bend
the wire, then wrap the ends of the
rouleau and wire with tape. Glue a
short length of narrow ribbon to
each of the shoe charms.

9 Cut five rose shapes from silk
using the design given in the
Templates section. Fold in half
lengthwise, and sew a gathering
thread close to the raw edges. Pull
the thread slightly, then roll up and
stitch securely at the gathered base.
Thread a length of regular wire
through the base of the bud, then
bend and twist the ends to form a
stem. Wrap the end of the bud and
wire in tape. Arrange the roses and
loops into a bunch with the leaves
around the edge.

10 Trim the stems with wire cutters, and wrap together with tape. Use the wire inside the leaves and loops to bend them into naturalistic shapes, and arrange them so that they frame the roses and fill in any spaces. Try to spread them evenly so that the white and cream colors are interspersed attractively. Tie the shoe charms with a small bow around the stem at the base of the flowers, then pin the corsage to the front of the bag.

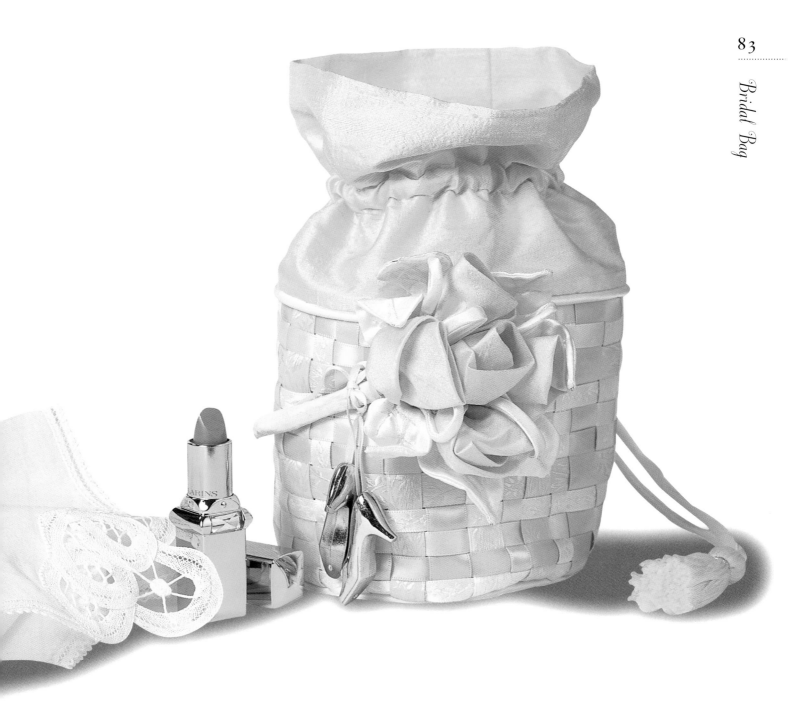

The Reception

The reception after the wedding service is an occasion for great celebration and the time when the two sets of families and friends can really get to know each other. It may be a small formal gathering over a gourmet meal, or a large and informal party with a buffet and dancing, but it is the attention to detail that the guests will enjoy and remember. Some of these projects, such as the favor bags and napkin rings, can be made well in advance, but others – the tablecloth and floral table centerpiece – can be saved until the final week.

Rose Confetti Box

The colorful tissue shapes of confetti may be cheerfully transient, but this useful handmade paper box, decked with a heart and rose, is a lasting reminder of a happy day.

CHOOSING YOUR MATERIALS

86

Throwing confetti – small pieces of paper cut into bows, petals, bells, and other lucky symbols – is a delightful way for the guests to greet the new bride and groom, and provides an excellent photo opportunity for the wedding pictures. Children can take part in the wedding preparations by helping to make environmentally friendly confetti by cutting up water soluble rice paper. They may even assist you with this easy-to-make and inexpensive confetti box. Remember that the size of the box can easily be varied. Beware of throwing colored confetti on a rainy day, however, as the colors may stain clothing.

YOU WILL NEED:

Graph paper
★
Heavyweight handmade paper with flower petals
★
Pencil and metal ruler
★
Double-sided adhesive tape
★
Pinking shears
★
30in (75cm) of ¾in (2cm) wide gold gauze ribbon
★
Silk rose and leaf spray
★
Craft glue
★
PROJECT TIME *1 hour*

1 Draw a pattern for the box on graph paper, following the outline in the Templates section and adjusting as required. Place this on the handmade paper, draw around it, and cut out.

2 Score along the fold lines indicated on the template using the blunt edge of a pair of scissors and a ruler.

Dried petals from roses and other brightly colored flowers can be used as a natural alternative to paper confetti, particularly in locations where there may be restrictions on its use.

3 Fold the card along the scored lines, as shown. Cut two strips of double-sided adhesive tape, and stick them to the side and bottom tabs. Peel off the backing paper from the tape, fold the card into the box shape, and press the adhesive tabs in place.

4 Cut out two heart shapes with pinking shears from the remaining paper, using the design in the Templates section. Stick in place on either side of the box where indicated on the template, using double-sided tape at each outside edge. Do not put any tape under the middle of the heart.

5 Thread the ribbon under the hearts and around the box. Fill the box with confetti and close by tying the ribbons into a bow. Finish off by taping a silk rose and leaf to one of the hearts.

Center of Attention

This floral table centerpiece makes a dramatic focal point for the head table at the reception. Not only is it eye-catching, but according to folklore, the variegated ivy leaves entwined around it symbolize wedded love and friendship.

CHOOSING YOUR MATERIALS

88

The arrangement of silk flowers and ribbon roses is built up on a woven wicker wreath. These are widely available from garden centers and florists, and come in various sizes and finishes, from the bleached wood used here to a darker, more rustic look. Although the flowers used should reflect the general decorative scheme of the wedding, they can be seasonal; blues and yellows for spring, pinks and reds for summer, or warm browns and russets for a fall wedding. Adding cream and white blooms and blossoms will give an unmistakably bridal look to any color combination.

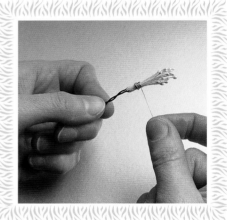

2 To make the center of the rose, fold the top of a length of wire across the middle of a small bunch of stamens. Fold the stamens in half, and bind in place with the wire from the ribbon.

YOU WILL NEED:

14in (36cm) lengths of medium wire for stems

★

Artificial stamens

★

1yd (90cm) of 1½in (4cm) wide wired ombré ribbon in 5 colors

★

1½yds (135cm) of ¾in (2cm) wide green wire-edged ribbon

★

Green sewing thread

★

5 silk rose leaves

★

12in (30cm) diameter wicker wreath

★

2 sprays of ivy

★

7 sprays of silk flowers in assorted colors and sizes

★

Wire cutters

★

Glue gun

★

PROJECT TIME *4 hours*

1 Knot one end of a length of wire-edge ribbon. Pulling gently on the wire at the other end, gather the ribbon into a ruffle. Wrap the wire around the loose end to secure, then trim.

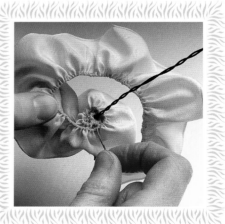

3 Wrap the knotted end of the ribbon around the stamens, and coil the ribbon around the center to form a rose. Secure with a few stitches as you build up the shape, then fold under the end and neaten. Bend the petals into shape.

4 Cut a 12in (30cm) length of green ribbon and gather one end. Wrap this around the base of the rose to form the calyx, then wind the rest down the length of the stem, stitching where necessary. Stitch a leaf securely to the stem, near the flower head. Make four more roses with the remaining wire-edged ribbons.

5 Cut the ivy into individual branches, and attach to the wreath. The ends can be pushed firmly into the garland to hold them in place, and the leaves tucked between the wicker strands.

6 Distribute the ribbon roses at regular intervals around the wreath. Fix in place with their wire stems, then use a glue gun to secure. Cut the other silk flowers into sprays and individual stems, and fix into the wreath. Glue a few large flowers on to fill in any spaces between the sprays.

89

Center of Attention

Bonbonnières

Delicate bonbonnières of organza and almonds are an increasingly popular addition to the wedding reception. They are so attractive that those guests who can resist eating the contents will often keep them as mementos.

CHOOSING YOUR MATERIALS

90

Quick and easy to make, bonbonnières consist of small bundles of sugared almonds tied up in a confection of ribbon, flowers, and organza. They can be arranged in ornamental baskets as table displays or distributed among the guests by the flower girl and ring bearer. Look for delicate, translucent fabrics and silk flowers that coordinate with your color scheme, and then add paper leaves and pearl sprays or lucky charms from cake-decorating suppliers.

YOU WILL NEED:

FOR EACH

★

10in (25cm) square of organza

★

10in (25cm) diameter plate

★

Pencil or dressmaker's pen

★

Three 20in (50cm) lengths of ⅛in (3mm) wide ribbon

★

2 silver or gold paper leaves

★

Silk flower and pearl spray

★

5 sugared almonds

★

Sewing thread

★

Basic sewing kit

★

PROJECT TIME *½ hour*

2 Place the almonds in the center of the organza and cup the fabric around them. Run a loose gathering thread around the almonds, then draw it up securely and secure the end.

1 Mark a circle onto the organza by drawing around the plate with either a pencil or a dressmaker's pen, whichever shows up best on your chosen fabric. Cut out around the drawn outline.

4 Add the paper leaves, silk flower and pearl spray, fixing them in place with a few stitches or glue. Vary the decorations on each bag to create an appealing display.

3 Holding the three lengths of ribbon together, tie them into a bow over the gathering thread.

Perfect Place Settings

Rich shades of warm metallic gold and bronze, offset by cool silver and lilac, combine to create a sumptuous atmosphere, ideal for a winter wedding. Each of the guests will feel especially welcome with an individual napkin ring and deliciously filled favor bag.

92

CHOOSING YOUR MATERIALS

This is an ideal project for people in a hurry, or those who have invited many people to the reception. It involves the minimal amount of stitching to produce a dramatic effect. Wide bands of gauzy or translucent ribbons can quickly be folded into small bags, filled with luxurious silvered and foil-wrapped almonds, and finished with extravagant bows. The matching napkin rings are made by binding wooden curtain rings with ribbon, but wider versions could be made using bands cut from a cardboard tube. A hand-lettered tag bearing each person's name could be tied around the neck of the favor bags to help the guests find their seats.

YOU WILL NEED:

FOR EACH NAPKIN RING

32in (80cm) of ¾in (2cm) wide
metallic ribbon
★
2½in (6cm) diameter curtain ring
★
24in (60cm) of ¾in (2cm) wide
gauze ribbon

FOR EACH BAG

12in (30cm) of 3in (8cm) wide
gauze ribbon
★
Gold, silver, and bronze
sugared almonds
★
16in (50cm) of ¾in (2cm) wide
metallic ribbon
★
Matching sewing thread
★
PROJECT TIME ½ hour each

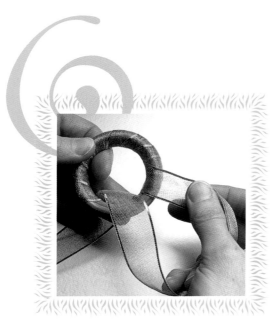

1 Remove the screw eye from the curtain ring if there is one. Secure one end of the metallic ribbon to the ring with a few stitches, and bind the rest tightly around at an angle. When it is completely covered, sew the other end in place and trim.

2 Tie gauze ribbon over the join, and secure with a few small stitches. Make the ribbon into a bow with short loops and long tails. Tie the tails again so that the bow now has four loops. Trim the ends neatly at an angle.

3 Fold the ribbon in half and pin the two sides together. Stitch along the outside edge, using matching thread and a small, neat running stitch. For speed, the edges could be sewn together by machine.

4 Fill the bag with almonds in a variety of colors. Gather up the open edge and tie the narrow length of ribbon into a bow around it.

Wedding Cake Tablecloth

A high point of the wedding reception is the moment when the first slice is cut from the cake. This flounced and flower-decked cloth will make sure that even the table on which it stands is dressed up for the occasion.

CHOOSING YOUR MATERIALS

The basic tablecloth is made from a length of inexpensive white cotton sheeting, with a full over-layer of fine, gauzy net. This is gathered up into deep flounces, swathed with translucent silver ribbons, and trimmed with swags of silk or fresh flowers. Pick colors that will complement, but not overwhelm, the cake's delicate icing and decorations. A double bow, with a matching floral spray, can be fixed to the handle of the cake knife. This idea can be adapted to fit any shape of table and would look particularly effective on a long buffet.

YOU WILL NEED:

1 rectangle of white cotton fabric and 1 rectangle of net; width = height of table, length = 2 x diameter of table, + 2in (5cm) all around for hems
★
Round piece of white cotton fabric to fit table top + 1½in (4cm) all around for hems
★
Matching sewing thread
★
Three 3yd (270cm) lengths of 2in (5cm) wide silver ribbons
★
4yds (350cm) of 2in (5cm) wide wire-edged ombré ribbon
★
1 yd (90cm) of 2in (4cm) wide white striped ribbon
★
3 sprays of artificial or fresh flowers
★
1 spray of silk orange blossom
★
Sewing machine
★
Basic sewing kit
★
PROJECT TIME **2 *hours***

1 Fold the round top piece into four and notch the quarters. Join the short ends of the skirt together to form a circle, then do the same with the net. Place the net over the cotton and pin together along the one edge. Fold into four and notch, then sew four gathering threads between the notches. With the net facing inward, pin the skirt to the top, matching the notches. Draw up the gathers to fit and pin.

2 Check the fit of the cloth over the table. Sew the skirt to the top, ¾in (2cm) from the outside edge, then trim the allowance to ¼in (6mm). Put the cloth back over the table and mark three equidistant points around the edge. At each mark, gather up the overskirt loosely into a swag and pin, 4in (10cm) from the top. Adjust the swags as necessary, then stab stitch in place.

5 Place a 24in (60cm) length of white striped ribbon centrally over the remaining wire-edged ribbon and tie the two together into a bow. Open out the loops and pull into shape. Gather each trailing end of white ribbon and sew to the center knot to form two more loops. Trim the ends of the colored ribbon into chevrons.

4 Cut three 40in (102cm) lengths of colored ribbon, tie into bows, and make into an attractive shape by bending the wire edges of the loops. Stitch securely over the streamers, then sew on the flower sprays to hang over the ribbons. (You may prefer to attach a bow and flowers to the front of the table only if it is to be placed in a corner.) Fresh flowers, which should be added at the very last minute, can be fixed on with lengths of raffia or florist's tape.

3 Pin one of the lengths of silver ribbon around the swags (you may need to adjust the length depending on the size of the table). Cut the other two pieces into 1yd (90cm) lengths and fold each in half. Pin, then stitch two lengths to the top of each gather to form streamers, then trim the ends.

6 Cut one large flower head from the sprays and stitch this to the knot. Separate out the orange blossoms and sew them around the center flower. Sew the remaining white ribbon to the back for tying the corsage onto the cake knife.

Wedding Cake Tablecloth

Treasured Memories

The wedding day itself is the culmination of months of careful and loving planning. Many people will have been involved along the way, united in their desire to make it a memorable and happy event for all those who attend. The bride and groom will wish to remember their individual contributions of time and friendship in future years. The miscellany of photographs, cards, invitations, letters, and gift wrappings can all be preserved and displayed, while the bridal gown, bouquet, and shoes can be stored away, ready to be handed on to a new generation as precious souvenirs.

Picture of Happiness

This double photograph frame can be used to display a favorite childhood snapshot alongside a portrait of the happy couple, and is an imaginative thank-you present for the bride and groom to give to their parents after the wedding.

YOU WILL NEED:

Two 8 x 10in (20 x 25cm)
rectangles of mountboard
★
Pencil and ruler
★
Craft knife and cutting board
★
Spray adhesive
★
9 x 22in (23 x 56cm) of batting
★
10 x 24in (50 x 60cm) of white silk
★
12 x 20in (30 x 50cm) of
cotton organdy
★
Fading pen
★
Machine or stranded embroidery
threads in pink and pale green
★
Scraps of guipure lace
★
Pink embroidery ribbon
★
Bronze metallic beads
★
Double-sided adhesive tape
★
Latex glue
★
3yds 6in (285cm) of narrow white
lace or pearl edging
★
Heavyweight handmade paper
★
Sewing machine
★
Basic sewing kit
★
PROJECT TIME *3 hours*

CHOOSING YOUR MATERIALS

The attractive textured look is achieved by combining three needlework techniques – lace appliqué, ribbon embroidery, and machine embroidery – worked onto a background of white silk. If your machine does not have preprogrammed stitches, you can sew the floral sprays with free stitching, or by hand. Cut the flower and leaf motifs from guipure lace, a machine-woven trimming, which has clearly defined motifs and does not fray. The design should be informal and unstructured; the precise shapes will depend on the lace and methods you use.

1 Draw a 3½ x 5½in (9 x 13cm) opening in the center of the mountboard rectangles and cut out using a craft knife and a cutting board. Cut the white silk into two pieces, each measuring 10 x 12in (25 x 30cm). Mark the outline of the frame onto each piece of silk with a fading pen. Cut the organdy into two 10 x 12in (25 x 30cm) pieces and baste one to the back of each marked silk rectangle.

2 With the fading pen, sketch in a trellis of leaves and roses in the areas to be embroidered. This will be around the lower left corner for the first frame and the top right corner for the second side. Machine or hand embroider the floral sprays in pink and green. The arrangement of the design should be loose and free-flowing rather than precisely and symmetrically arranged.

3 Cut out the most interesting flower shapes from the lace, and stitch in place by hand or machine. Concentrate the larger flowers around the corners to give structure to your design. Fill in the spaces with loosely worked French knots in pink ribbon, then sew clusters of beads in any remaining spaces and to the centers of some of the lace flowers.

4 Cut the batting into two 9 x 11in (23 x 28cm) rectangles and fix to the front of the boards with spray adhesive. Cut the surplus away from the openings and the edges. Carefully cut two diagonals across the unworked center of each embroidered silk piece and place face down. Lay the padded side of the frame on top, matching the corners. Fold the loose triangles to the back and secure with double-sided adhesive tape.

5 Attach the narrow lace around the inner and outer edges of each frame with latex glue, neatening the joins carefully. Fix your chosen photographs in place on the back of the mountboard with narrow strips of double-sided adhesive tape.

6 Cut a 10 x 16½in (25 x 42cm) rectangle of heavyweight handmade paper. Tape one frame to each end of the paper, leaving a space in the middle to form a hinge.

Wedding Dress Box

There will be many cherished memories surrounding the bride's wedding gown, so it must be safeguarded with care. Instead of keeping it on a hanger, fold the dress carefully and store in this ribbon-bound box, along with a fragrant lavender sachet.

CHOOSING YOUR MATERIALS

A simple yet sturdy cardboard container can be turned into an attractive storage box by covering it with brocade and making a satin lining. When the dress is folded, it should be interleaved with sheets of museum quality acid- and dye-free tissue paper (available from good stationery suppliers) to protect the fabric from becoming heavily creased or marked. The box is tied with two flamboyant flowered bows, and should be kept in a cool, dark place, well away from drafts or dampness.

2 Open out the fabric at the corners and cut away the excess to within ½in (15mm) of the pins. Refold and glue the short ends neatly in place. Trim the overlapping edges of the fabric so that they are level with the rim.

YOU WILL NEED:

Large cardboard box with lid
★
Lightweight textured paper
★
Craft glue
★
Thin cardboard
★
Cream fabric to cover lid
★
White satin for lining the box and lid
★
Latex glue
★
Length of ½in (15mm) wide gold ribbon, to fit around the rim + 1½in (4cm) for hems
★
2 lengths of ½in (4cm) wide floral or gold spangled wire-edged ribbon to tie around the box
★
PROJECT TIME *2 hours*

1 Remove the lid, then cover the rest of the box with textured paper, glued in place. Leave the inside base unpapered. Cut a piece of cream fabric large enough to cover the top and rim of the lid, plus ¾in (2cm) all around. Apply latex glue sparingly to the top of the lid and stick the fabric centrally on top, then glue the fabric to the long edges. Neatly fold under the fabric at each corner and mark the crease lines with pins.

3 Cut two strips of fabric to line the inside rim of the lid, each measuring the length of one long and one short side, plus 3in (8cm). The width should equal the depth of the lid, plus ¾in (2cm). Pin a 1cm (15mm) pleat ¾in (2cm) from one short end of each strip.

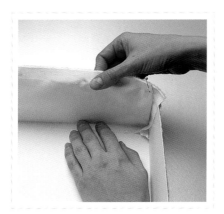

Wedding Dress Box

4 Turn the lid upside down. Place the first strip of lining so that the pleat lies at one corner, and with latex glue, stick the long edge to the base of the lid, keeping the fabric flat against the side. When you reach the next corner, make another ½in (15mm) pleat. Fold under ½in (2cm) at the pleated end of the second strip and glue it along the two remaining sides. Fold under the end of the strip to neaten, and glue in position. The pleats form neat, tidy corners.

5 Pin the raw edge of the lining back over the edge of the lid, snipping the corners so that the fabric lies flat. Glue in place along the outside rim. Starting at the center of one side, glue gold ribbon around the rim to cover the raw edges of the lining. Turn under the end of the ribbon and glue it on top of the raw end to make a neat join. Line the inside edge of the main box in the same way.

6 Cut two rectangles of thin cardboard to fit inside the box and lid, and cut two pieces of lining fabric to fit, each ¾in (2cm) larger all around than the card. Stick the edges to the underside of the card with latex glue, mitering the corners neatly, as shown. Glue in place inside the box and lid. Wrap the dress in tissue and place inside the box. Put on the lid, then tie two lengths of wire-edged ribbon around the box, finishing each off in a bow.

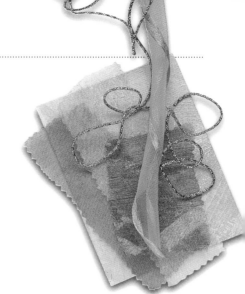

LeMoyne Star Sachet

This lavender bag is too attractive to keep hidden away in the wedding-dress box, for the traditional American LeMoyne patchwork block is made up in unexpected fabrics – a selection of rich metallic organzas.

YOU WILL NEED:

Graph paper
★
Pencil and ruler
★
Thin cardboard
★
Glue
★
Paper scissors
★
Rotary cutter (optional)
★
4 x 8in (8 x 20cm) each of bronze and light silver organza
★
8 x 10in (20 x 25cm) of dark silver organza
★
16in (40cm) of 1½in (4cm) wide gauze ribbon
★
Dried lavender
★
Short length of narrow gold cord (optional)
★
Matching sewing thread
★
Sewing machine
★
Basic sewing kit
★
PROJECT TIME *3 hours*

CHOOSING YOUR MATERIALS

Lavender bushes are cultivated in many town and country gardens for their characteristic scent, which can easily be preserved. Cut the stems while still in bud, then hang upside down in a cool place to dry out. The flower heads can then be used to fill small fabric bags which will ward off moths and give out a long-lasting aromatic perfume. These translucent fabrics allow the color of the lavender to show through, giving a memorable effect.

1 Make the four templates by copying the patchwork block given in Techniques & Templates onto graph paper. Glue it onto thin cardboard and cut out pieces A, B, C, and D. Using scissors or a rotary cutter, cut out four diamonds from shape A in bronze, four from shape B in light silver, and four each from C and D in dark silver organza.

2 Assemble the star by pinning one piece A and one piece B together with right sides facing. Stitch together ¼in (6mm) from the long edge, and press the seam allowance to one side. Make another pair to match. Pin the two pairs together, carefully matching the center seams; stitch, and press as before.

3 To set in the corner squares (shape C), pin and stitch one side to the outside edge of one diamond, matching the raw edges and corner points. Swivel the square to line up with the next diamond, then pin and stitch together. Press the seam allowance to one side. Set in the triangle (shape D) in the same way. Make up the second part of the square. Matching the center point, stitch the two halves together, then complete by setting in the remaining two triangles.

4 Cut the ribbon into four equal lengths to make the corner trims. Fold each piece in half, and tie into a knot. Matching the raw edges, pin one trim to each corner of the finished block, and stitch in place, ¼in (6mm) from the edge. For the backing, cut a 4in (10cm) square from dark silver organza. With right sides together, pin to the front, and stitch together around three of the sides. Press the seam allowance on the fourth side to the wrong side. Turn right side out.

5 Cut two 4in (10cm) squares from the remaining organza to make the inner lining. Pin and stitch together ⅓in (8mm) from the outside edge, leaving a small gap in the fourth side. Make a funnel from a rolled piece of paper. Insert the point of the funnel into the gap and fill the lining with dried lavender. Close the gap with slip stitch.

6 If desired, sew a length of gold cord to the center of the star. Use this to attach a lucky charm, to hang the sachet, or simply for decoration. Insert the scented sachet into the main bag, and slip stitch the fourth side closed.

Drawstring Shoe Bag

Most brides will wear their new wedding shoes only once, and many have been treasured and survived to be handed down as family heirlooms. Keep your wedding slippers or a special pair of shoes in pristine condition by storing them safely in this drawstring bag.

CHOOSING YOUR MATERIALS

Remember that all shoes, whether satin or leather, should be cleaned as necessary and fitted with shoe-trees to prevent them becoming misshapen. Then wrap each one carefully in tissue paper before putting them away. The bag is made from soft waffle-weave fabric – a small cotton hand-towel would be ideal – and trimmed with an elegant white-shoe motif. You could make a second version for the bride's trousseau, to hold her going-away shoes while she is on her honeymoon.

YOU WILL NEED:

16 x 22in (40 x 55cm) of white textured cotton fabric

★

6 x 22in (16 x 55cm) of striped floral cotton fabric

★

4 x 6in (10 x 15cm) of white cotton drill

★

26in (65cm) of ¾in (2cm) wide broderie-anglaise lace edging

★

4 x 6in (10 x 15cm) of fusible web

★

4in (10cm) of ⅜in (1cm) wide satin ribbon

★

1yd (90cm) of 1in (2.5cm) wide ribbon for drawstring

★

Pencil

★

Safety pin

★

Sewing machine

★

Basic sewing kit

★

PROJECT TIME *2 hours*

1 Cut a 2½ x 22in (6 x 55cm) strip of textured cotton fabric and a 3 x 22in (8 x 55cm) strip of flowered cotton. With right sides facing, sew the flowered strip to the remaining large piece of textured cotton, ½in (15mm) in from one long edge. To make the drawstring channel, press under ½in (15mm) at each short end of the textured fabric strip, then press in half lengthwise with wrong sides together. Pin and stitch the raw edges to the floral strip, starting ½in (15mm) in from the edge.

2 Using the cutting diagram in Techniques & Templates as a guide, cut the remaining floral fabric into four pieces, and join together along the diagonal edges to form a 9 x 7in (23 x 18cm) rectangle. Press the seams flat. The space in the center will be covered by the motif.

3 Draw the shoe motif from Techniques & Templates onto the fusible web, cut out, and fix to the center of the rectangle with a cool iron. Press under a ½in (15mm) turning along each side, clipping the surplus fabric so that the corners lie flat.

4 Using satin stitch and white thread, sew around the outline of the shoe and along the stitching line marked on the template. Slip stitch the broderie-anglaise around the outside edge of the rectangle, to form a frame. Start stitching 1½in (4cm) in from the edge and miter each corner, sewing across the diagonal fold formed on the underside and trimming the seams.

5 Fold the bag in half widthwise with right sides facing. Pin and stitch the bottom and side together as far as the casing, ½in (15mm) from the edge. Trim back the seam allowance and neaten with a zigzag. Clip the corners and turn right side out. Sew the motif rectangle to the center front. Make a bow from the narrow ribbon and stitch to the front of the shoe.

6 Pin the safety pin to one end of the wide ribbon and thread through the drawstring channel. Tie the ends securely together in a knot and trim.

Keepsake Box

A plain cardboard box can be stenciled with this nostalgic design of apple blossoms and bows to make an attractive storage place for greetings cards, photographs, cake decorations, videos, and other precious wedding mementos.

CHOOSING YOUR MATERIALS

There are many different-sized storage boxes to be found in stationers, department stores, and interiors shops. By enlarging or reducing the template on a photocopier, the stencil can easily be adapted to fit your chosen box. Instead of cutting the design from cardboard, which does take some time, you may prefer to use the clear plastic sheets and cutting tools available from most specialty stores. When stenciling the design, use only the minimum amount of paint on the brush. Apply it with a gentle circling movement, keeping the brush upright to give a clean outline to the shapes.

YOU WILL NEED:

Cardboard storage box
★
White acrylic primer or gesso
★
1in (2.5cm) wide paintbrush
★
Stencil card
★
Carbon paper
★
Cutting mat
★
Sharp knife
★
Repositionable spray adhesive
★
Medium and small stencil brushes
★
Stencil paints in yellow gold and light and dark shades of pink, green, and blue
★
Clear matte spray varnish
★
PROJECT TIME 5 *hours*

1 Paint the box and its lid with several coats of acrylic primer or gesso to give a smooth, flat surface. Allow to dry thoroughly.

2 Adjust the design from the Templates section to the size required. Transfer it onto the stencil card with carbon paper. Cut away the card within the outlines with a sharp knife, working on a cutting mat. Always hold the knife firmly and cut away from yourself. Work slowly, especially around intricate details such as the flower centers.

Keepsake Box

5 Stencil the ribbons in pale blue, then give depth to the design with dark blue shadows.

4 Fill in the flower centers with yellow stencil paint. Color the leaves in light green, then add dark green highlights.

3 Attach the stencil to the box lid with a light coat of spray adhesive, following the manufacturer's instructions. Using a medium brush, stencil the flowers in light pink paint. Allow the paint to dry before applying the next color. Add a dark pink rim to the petals with a fine brush.

6 Carefully remove the stencil, and when the paint is quite dry, protect the surface with several coats of clear matte varnish. Follow the manufacturer's instructions when using this, and as with the spray adhesive, make sure the room is well ventilated.

Découpage Souvenir Tray

Collect together the variety of ephemera that will accumulate during the wedding period – each carrying special memories – to make this colorful découpage tray. This decorative artifact may well become a family heirloom.

CHOOSING YOUR MATERIALS

Along with the cards, letters, and telegrams that the newly married couple will want to keep, there will inevitably be many other bits and pieces – printed wrapping paper, confetti, gift tags, and even cake decorations. Sort out the most attractive pieces that complement each other, and stick onto a wooden tray base. Coat them with several layers of protective varnish to make a lasting souvenir. You could also use the same technique to cover the lid of a box, a lamp base, or even the door of a small cupboard.

YOU WILL NEED:

Small wooden tray
★
Fine sandpaper
★
Silver craft paint
★
Pearlized craft paint
★
Large paintbrush
★
Stencil brush
★
Silver paper cake band
★
Silver paper leaves
★
Wrapping paper, confetti, printed scraps, and so on
★
Craft glue
★
Clear acrylic varnish
★
PROJECT TIME 3 *hours*

1 Sand down the tray to give a smooth working surface, then coat with two layers of silver paint. When completely dry, apply the pearlized paint with a stencil brush, using a stippling movement to create a raised texture.

2 Cut four lengths from the silver cake band to fit along each side of the tray, and glue in place. Glue a large silver leaf over each of the corner joins.

3 Sort through the souvenirs and cut out interesting motifs – cherubs, cakes, and hearts. Use your imagination to make a really individual arrangement.

4 Glue the shapes down, taking care not to tear them. When the design is complete, seal the découpage with a further thin layer of glue, making sure there are no air bubbles caught beneath the paper shapes.

5 Finish off with several layers of gloss acrylic varnish to give a lasting and waterproof surface.

Découpage Souvenir Tray

Techniques & Templates

The projects in this book cover a wide range of craft methods – découpage, stenciling, and flower arranging – all of which are shown in detail within the project instructions. Most of the needlework and embroidery terms will be familiar to anyone with a basic knowledge of sewing, but they are explained here, to help give your work a professional finish. Many of the projects also require templates, and these are supplied here with clear instructions for use.

BASIC SEWING KIT

The following items should be in every well-stocked work box: **embroidery scissors** with long pointed blades and **dressmaking shears** that are kept for cutting fabric only. Scissors are a long-term investment, so it is worth buying an expensive pair. **Dressmaker's pins** come in various lengths and thicknesses; brass lace-making pins are good for fine fabrics, but pearly- or glass-headed pins are less awkward to use and show up well. You will also need a **tape measure** and a selection of **needles** ranging from a fine size 10 for beading to embroidery, tapestry, and general sewing needles. A good **steam iron** and a large **ironing board** are vital for finishing seams and pressing. Many of the projects require a **sewing machine**; a well-maintained basic swing-needle model that can produce an even zigzag and straight stitch is all that is needed.

Sewing Techniques

BIAS STRIPS

Cutting fabric on the bias, or across the grain, gives it extra flexibility so that it can be curved neatly. Fold the corner of the fabric at 45 degrees, so that the end of the fabric meets one edge. Press along this diagonal and unfold. Mark a parallel line the required width away from the crease and cut out the strip.

ROULEAUX

To make a rouleau, fold a narrow bias strip in half lengthwise and stitch together ¼in (6mm) from the outside edge. Fasten the loose ends of the sewing thread securely to a tapestry needle, and thread the needle back through. Ease it gently along, so that the fabric turns back on itself to form a tube.

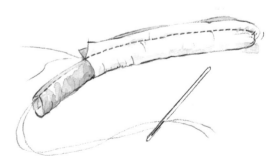

FUSIBLE WEB

Iron-on fusible web is a quick method of fixing a shape to a background fabric. Trace the motif onto the paper side of the web, remembering that the image will be reversed. Cut out roughly, and with a warm iron, fix to the wrong side of the appliqué fabric. Cut the motif out around the outline and peel off the backing paper. With the adhesive side downward, place onto the main fabric and iron in place.

SINGLE HEMS

Thick fabrics are finished with a single hem that has just one turning. Neaten the raw edge with zigzag stitch or with pinking shears, fold to the wrong side of the fabric, then pin and stitch in place by hand or machine.

DOUBLE HEMS

A double hem should be used for a fine fabric. Press under ¼in (6mm) along the raw edge, then turn over another ½in (16mm). Pin, then hand or machine stitch ⅛in (3mm) from the fold.

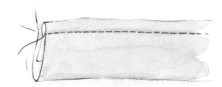

Sewing Stitches

BASTING STITCH

This is a temporary stitch to hold two pieces of fabric together before they are hemmed or seamed. It should be worked in a contrasting thread that can easily be unpicked. The stitches and spaces should be equal and can vary from ¼ to ½in (6mm to 12mm) apart.

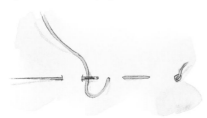

BUTTONHOLE STITCH

This can be used as an edging stitch or for free embroidery. A row of regular upright stitches is worked from left to right, with the thread always passing below the needle.

BUTTONHOLE LOOPS

These are made by working a row of closely spaced buttonhole stitches over a bar formed from several long straight stitches.

OVER STITCH

This is used to finish off an edge or to join two edges together. It is worked over the edge in the fabric in a series of straight diagonal stitches, spaced at regular intervals.

SLIP STITCH

This stitch is used to join two folded edges. Butt the edges together and bring the needle out through the one of the folds, then into the other fold. Make a ¼in (6mm) stitch within that fold, then bring the needle out and back into the opposite fold. Take care not to not pull the thread too tightly.

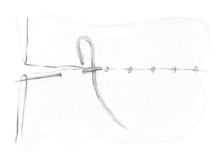

STAB STITCH

This joins one piece of fabric to another invisibly and can be used to attach hat bands or bows. Bring the needle through to the right side, then insert it back, close to the point where it emerged. Continue, making a series of small stitches that can be close or widely spaced.

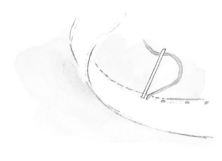

Embroidery Stitches

CROSS STITCH

A cross stitch is formed by two diagonal stitches, which cross each other at a right angle. It can be worked individually, ideal for outlines and lettering, or in rows as shown, which is a quicker way to cover large areas. The top stitches should be worked in the same direction to give an even finish.

FEATHER STITCH

This is worked in a series of alternate diagonal stitches, from top to bottom. The thread should pass under the needle each time it is drawn through, to create the characteristic loops. It can be worked either in a neat row, or more freely to give an open, fern-like appearance.

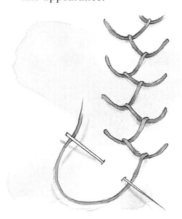

FRENCH KNOTS

These are used as a filling stitch, or singly as a highlight. Bring the needle through, and holding the thread taut with your other hand, twist the needle around it two or three times. Insert the needle back through the fabric, close to the point from which it emerged, and draw through to form a knot.

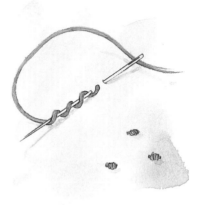

HERRINGBONE STITCH

This forms a band of overlapping diagonal stitches. They are worked in alternate directions, from left to right, with a regular space left between each one.

LAZY DAISY STITCH

This stitch is often used to form flower and leaf motifs. The single stitches can be worked so that they radiate from a central point. Bring the needle through to the right side and insert it back at the same point. Bring it through to the right side again with the loop of thread under the point of the needle. Draw the needle through and hold the loop down with a small straight stitch.

SPLIT STITCH

This is an outline stitch that can also be worked in closely spaced rows as a smooth-surfaced filling stitch. The needle passes through the thread each time it is brought through, so that the individual stitches are not visible.

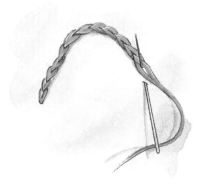

Templates

Unless stated otherwise, the templates are shown full size. In these cases, simply trace or photocopy the template and then use as described in the main instructions. Sometimes, however, the templates have been reduced in size. In such instances, there are two options open to you. The first is to enlarge the template using a photocopier. To do this, set the photocopier to enlarge by the appropriate percentage, which is clearly indicated next to the template. The second option is to trace the template onto graph paper and then to scale it up by copying the design, square by square, onto another piece of graph paper with a grid of larger squares. The grid sizes you should use are clearly indicated next to the template. Occasionally, you will have to experiment. For example, the Keepsake Box template on page 119 will need to be scaled up or down depending on the particular size and shape of the box you choose to decorate. It is easiest to do this on a photocopier.

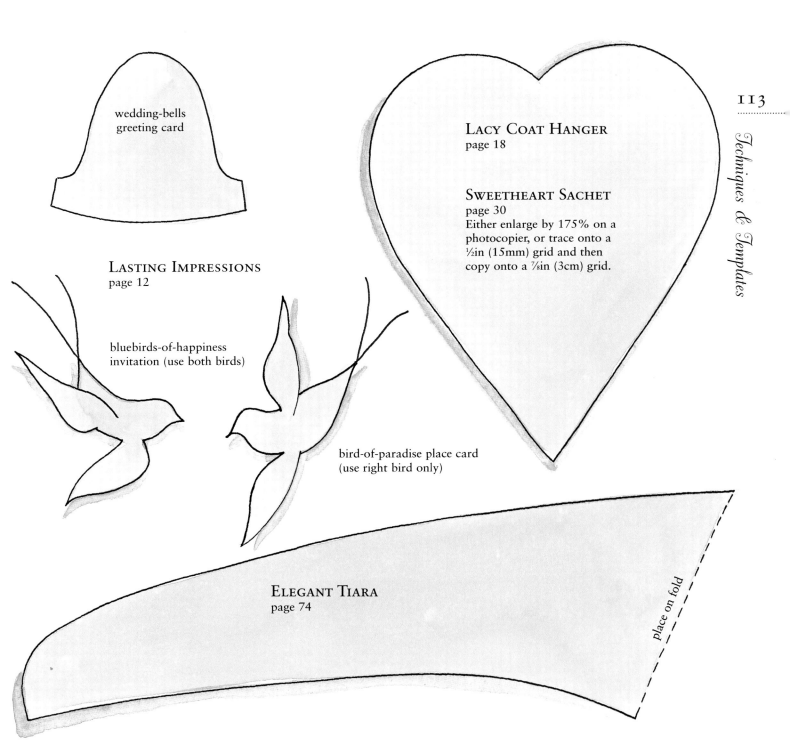

wedding-bells greeting card

LASTING IMPRESSIONS
page 12

bluebirds-of-happiness invitation (use both birds)

bird-of-paradise place card (use right bird only)

LACY COAT HANGER
page 18

SWEETHEART SACHET
page 30
Either enlarge by 175% on a photocopier, or trace onto a ½in (15mm) grid and then copy onto a ⅞in (3cm) grid.

ELEGANT TIARA
page 74

place on fold

BOX OF DELIGHTS
page 16

French knot clusters

Lazy daisy stitch leaves

Roses

Lazy daisy stitch rosebuds

Gorgeous Gifts
page 22

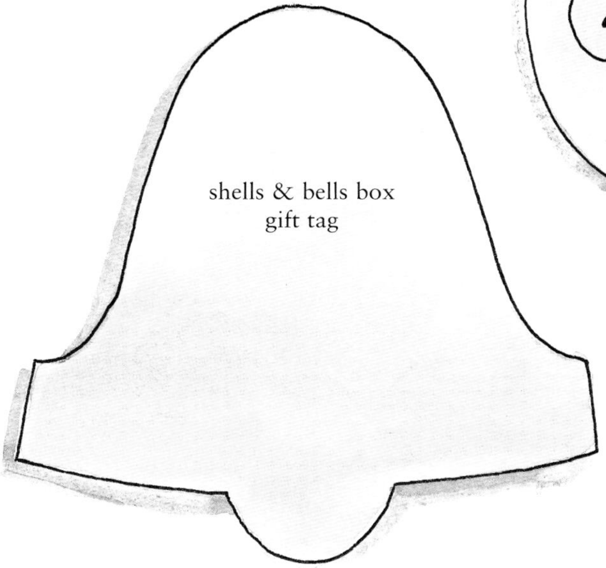
shells & bells box
gift tag

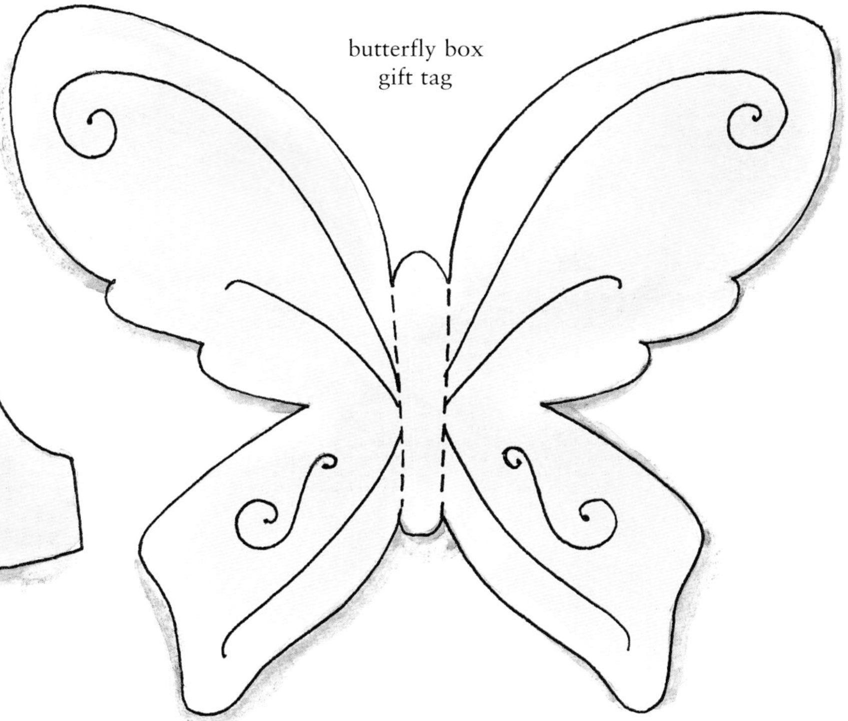
butterfly box
gift tag

Sweet Dreams
page 36

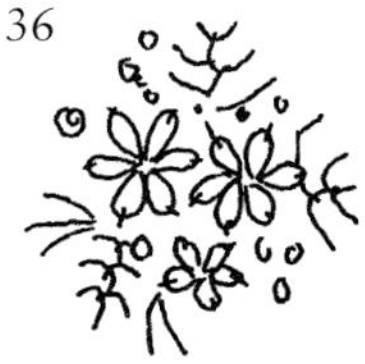

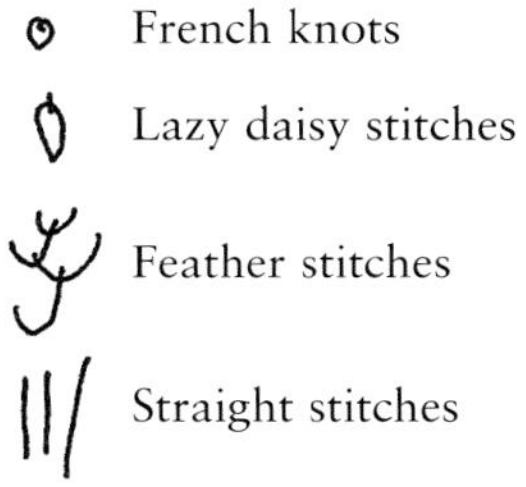
French knots
Lazy daisy stitches
Feather stitches
Straight stitches

Beaded Hat Pin
page 42

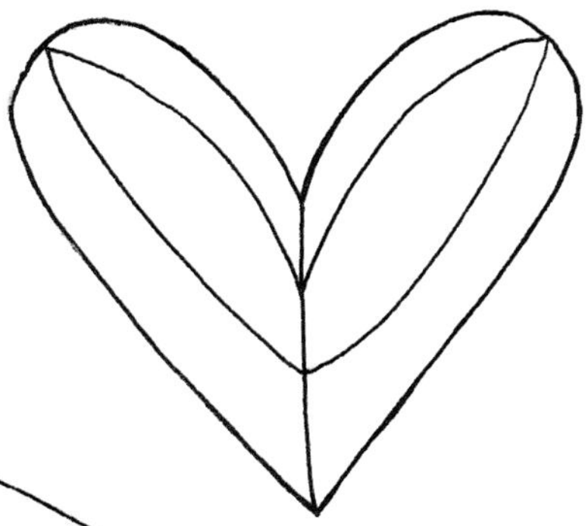

Bridal Bag
page 80

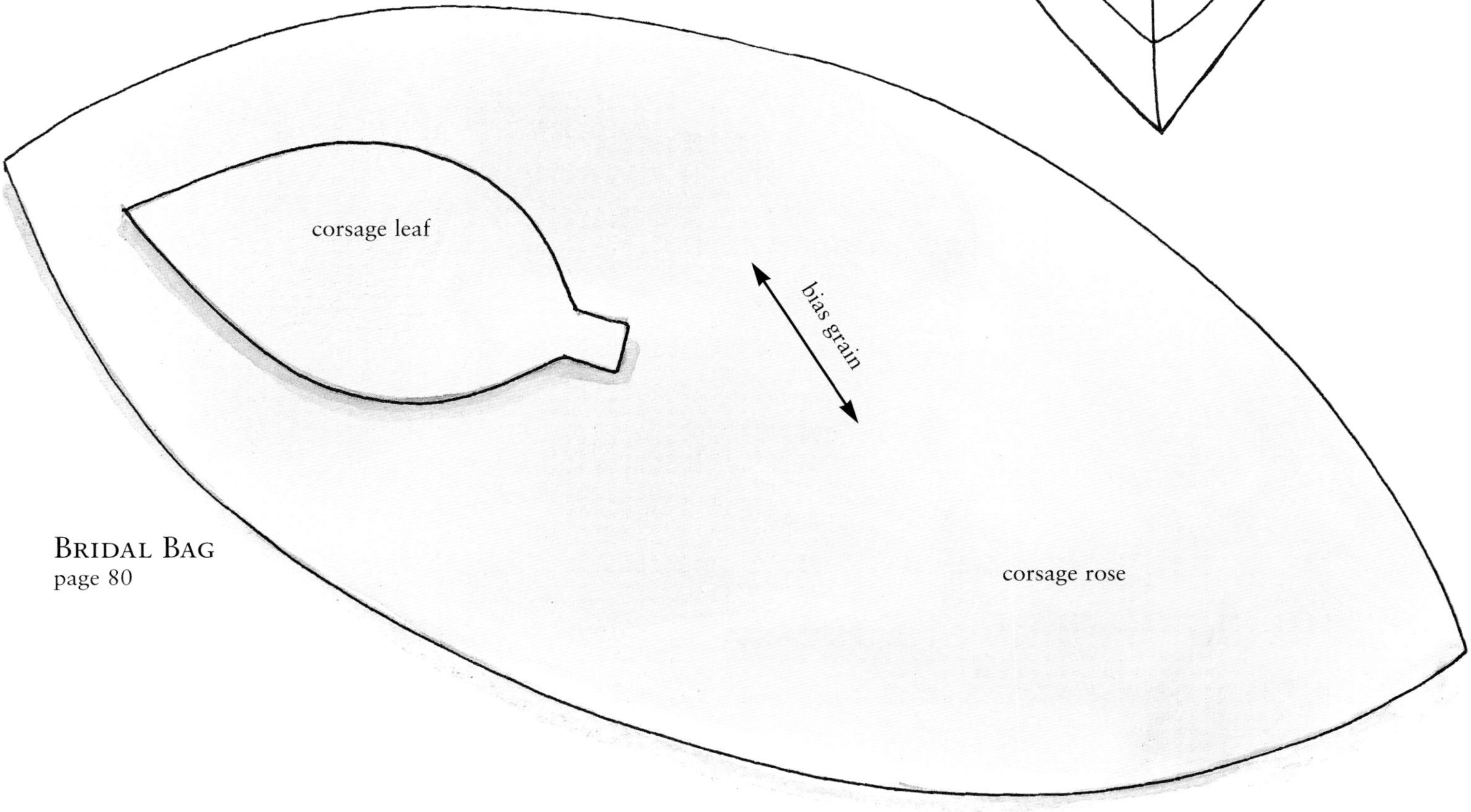
corsage leaf
bias grain
corsage rose

Techniques & Templates

A B C D E F G H

I J K L M N O P

Q R S T U V W X

Y Z

LOVE-BIRDS PILLOW
page 32
Either enlarge by 175% on a photocopier, or trace onto
a ½in (15mm) grid and then copy onto a ⅞in (3cm) grid.

Techniques & Templates

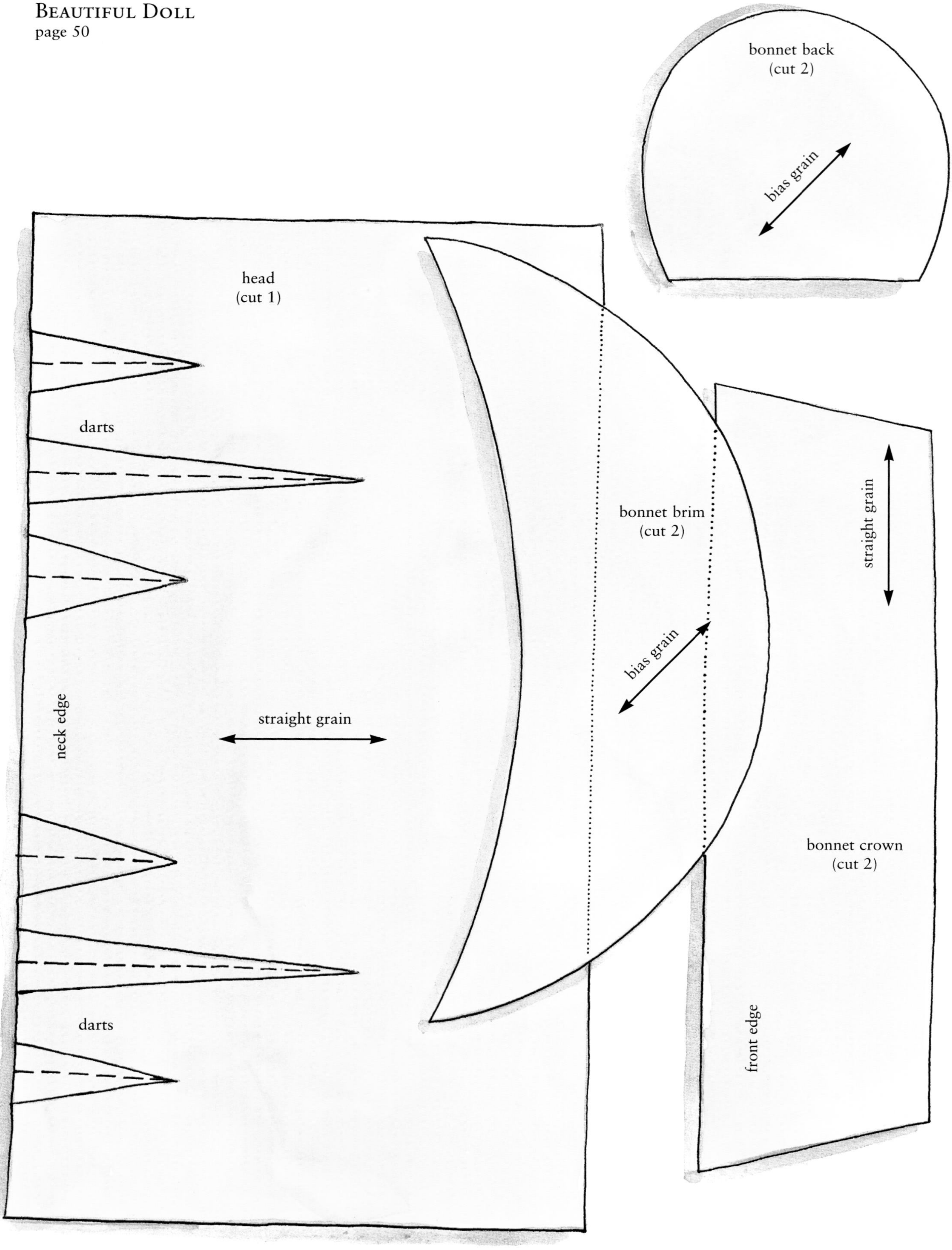

bonnet back
(cut 2)

bias grain

head
(cut 1)

Techniques & Templates

darts

bonnet brim
(cut 2)

straight grain

neck edge

bias grain

straight grain

bonnet crown
(cut 2)

darts

front edge

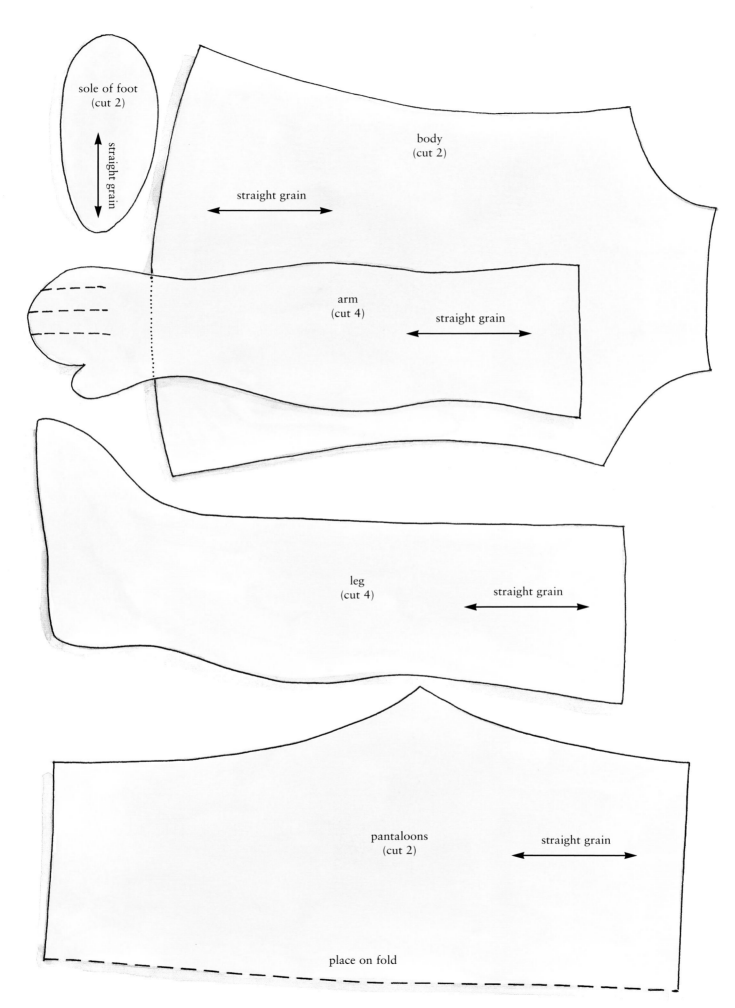

sole of foot
(cut 2)

straight grain

body
(cut 2)

straight grain

arm
(cut 4)

straight grain

leg
(cut 4)

straight grain

pantaloons
(cut 2)

straight grain

place on fold

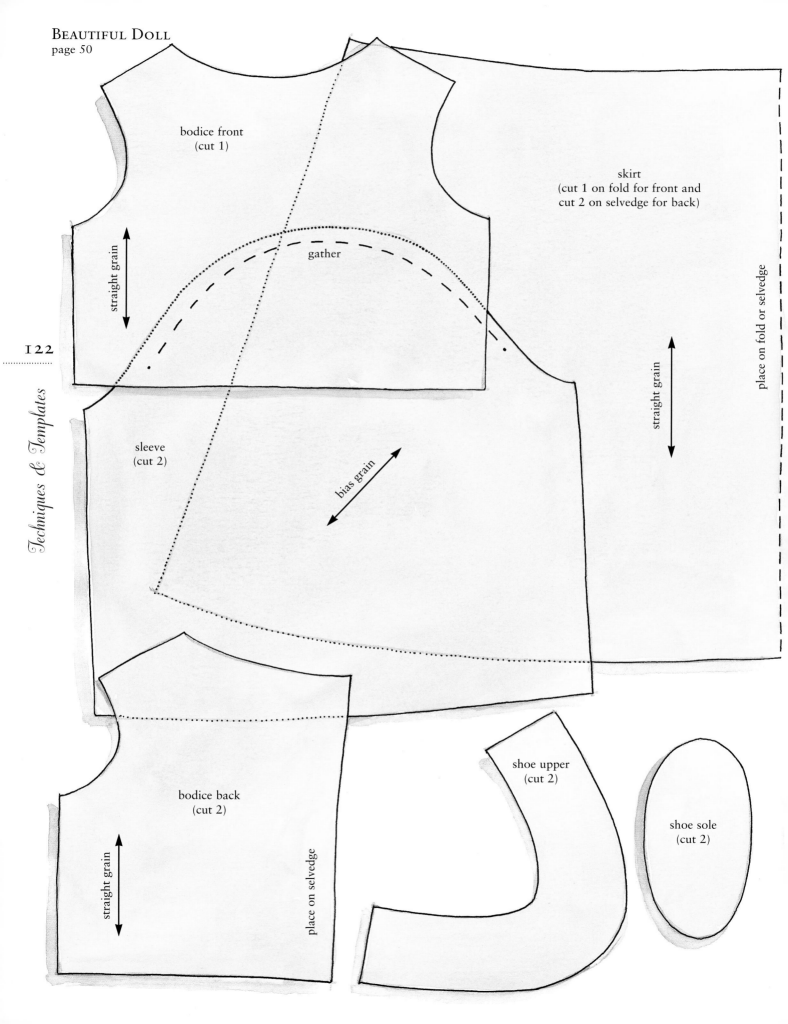

bodice front
(cut 1)

skirt
(cut 1 on fold for front and
cut 2 on selvedge for back)

straight grain

gather

place on fold or selvedge

straight grain

122

Techniques & Templates

sleeve
(cut 2)

bias grain

bodice back
(cut 2)

straight grain

place on selvedge

shoe upper
(cut 2)

shoe sole
(cut 2)

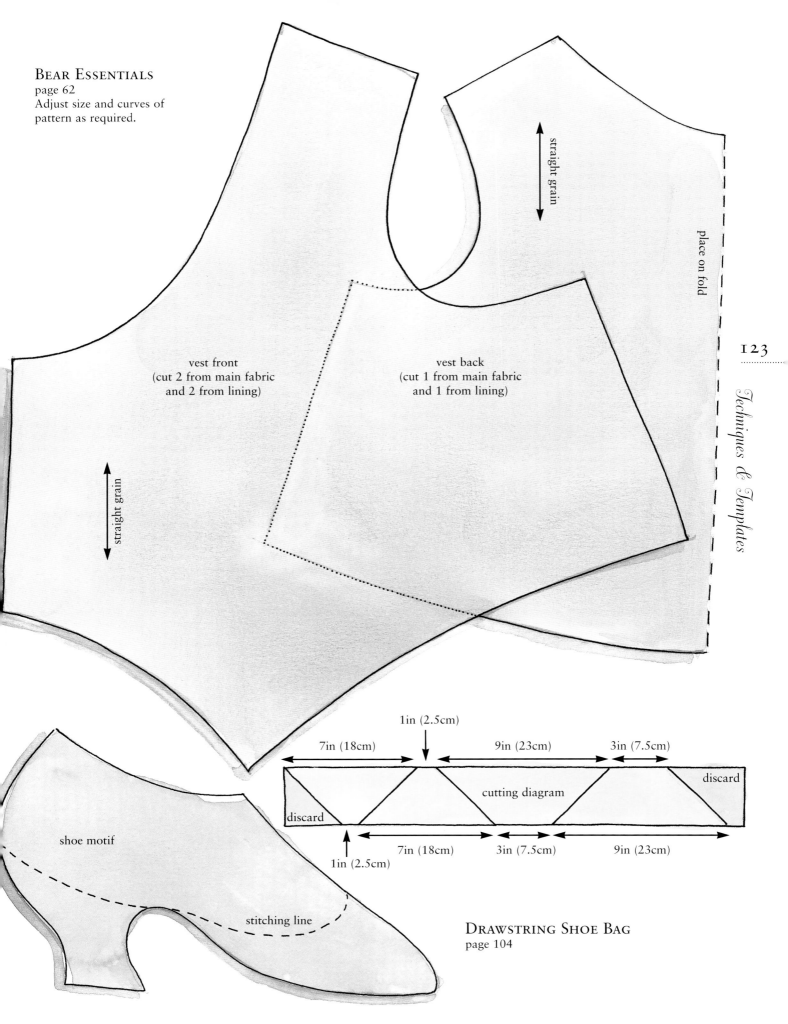

BEAR ESSENTIALS
page 62
Adjust size and curves of
pattern as required.

straight grain

place on fold

vest front
(cut 2 from main fabric
and 2 from lining)

vest back
(cut 1 from main fabric
and 1 from lining)

straight grain

shoe motif

stitching line

1in (2.5cm)

7in (18cm)   9in (23cm)   3in (7.5cm)

discard

cutting diagram

discard

7in (18cm)   3in (7.5cm)   9in (23cm)

1in (2.5cm)

DRAWSTRING SHOE BAG
page 104

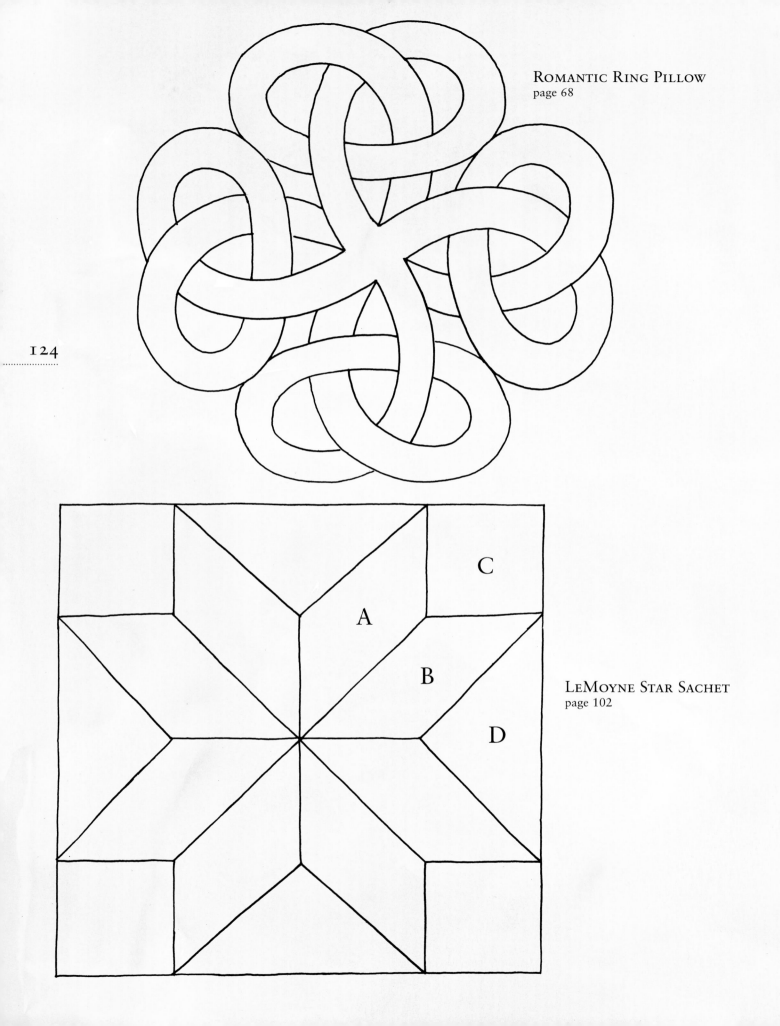

ROMANTIC RING PILLOW
page 68

124

LeMoyne Star Sachet
page 102

A

B

C

D

Rose Confetti Box

page 86
The size and proportions
can be adjusted
as required.

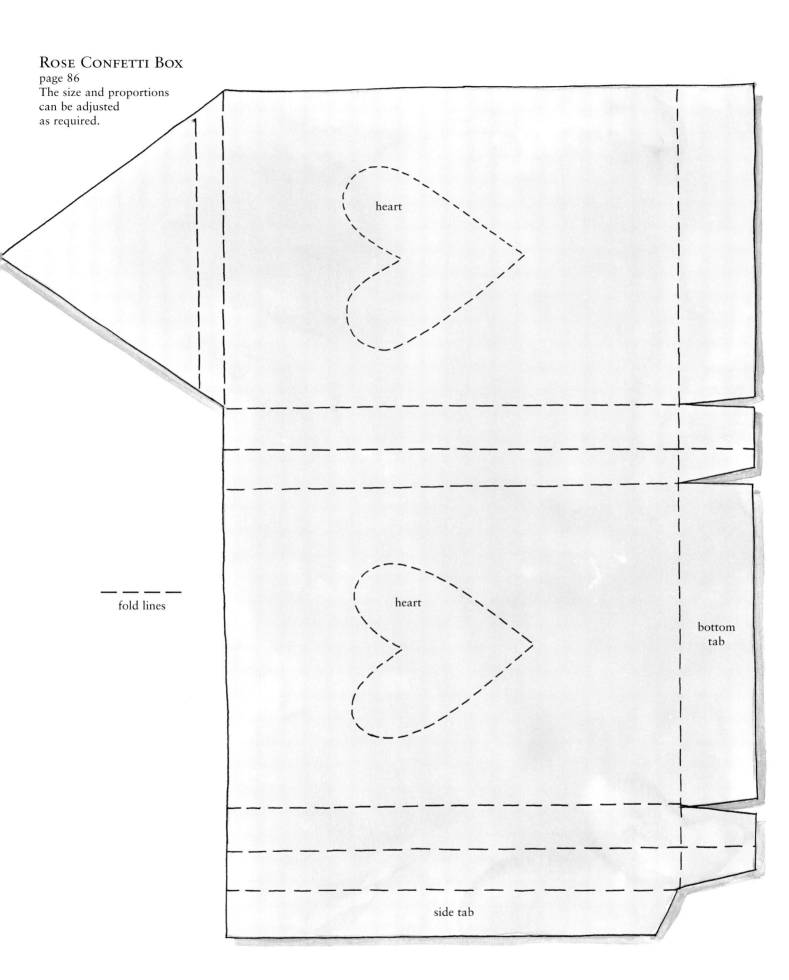

heart

heart

fold lines

bottom
tab

side tab

Index

A
albums of love 14–15

B
bags:
  bridal 80–3
    templates 115
  favor 92–3
  shoe 104–5
    templates 123
basket, for perfume and cosmetics 20–1
basting stitch 111
beaded hat pin 42–3
  template 115
bear essentials 62–3
  templates 123
beautiful doll 50–3
  templates 120–2
beauty basket 20–1
beauty treatments 9
bias strips 110
bird-of-paradise place card 13
  template 113
bluebirds-of-happiness
  invitation 13
    templates 113
bonbonnières 90–1
bouquet, bridal 78–9
bow tie and cummerbund,
  for young ring bearer 60–1
boxes:
  butterfly 24
    template 115
  confetti 86–7
    templates 125
  Cupid's heart 25
  of delights 16–17
    templates 114
  heart-shaped, for jewelry
    16–17
    templates 114
  keepsake 106–7
    template 119
  pretty pinks 23
  rose and organza 22
  shells and bells 25
  for wedding dress 100–1
bridal attendants 7

bow tie and cummerbund for
    60–1
  gifts for 50–3, 62–3
  headdress for 58–9
  slippers for 56–7
  Victorian cornucopia for 54–5
bridal bag 80–3
  templates 115
bridesmaids' outfits 8
  headdress 58–9
  slippers 56–7
butterfly box 24
  template 115
buttonhole loops 111
buttonhole stitch 111

C
center of attention 88–9
centerpiece, table 88–9
ceremony, arranging 7
Cinderella slippers 56–7
circlet of flowers 58–9
coat hanger, lacy 18–19
  template 113
confetti box 86–7
  templates 125
cornucopia, Victorian lace-trimmed
    54–5
cross stitch 112
crowning glory 76–7
cummerbund and bow tie,
  for young ring bearer 60–1
Cupid's heart box 25

D
découpage souvenir tray 108–9
doll, miniature flower girl 50–3
  templates 120–2
double hems 111
drawstring shoe bag 104–5
  templates 123

E
elegant tiara 74–5
  template 113
embroidery stitches 112
everlasting bouquet 78–9

F
feather stitch 112
floral garland 58–9
flower girl doll 50–3
  templates 120–2
flowers, for ceremony 7
French knots 112
fusible web 111

G
garland, floral 58–9
garter: lace, bead, and sequin 72–3
gift boxes:
  butterfly 24
    template 115
  Cupid's heart 25
  pretty pinks 23
  rose and organza 22
  shells and bells 25
gifts:
  for friends and family 8
  wedding, registering at store 8
  for wedding party 39–63
good luck garter 72–3
greeting cards:
  jeweled-heart 12
  wedding-bells 12
    template 113
groom, vest for 66–7

H
hair decoration, posy 48–9
handkerchief, lace-edged 40–1
hat pin, beaded 42–3
  template 1115
hat trick 44–7
hats, decorating 44–7
headdresses:
  floral band 76–7
  tiara 74–5
    template 113
heirloom sampler 28–9
  template 116
hems:
  double 111
  single 111
herringbone stitch 112
honeymoon 8–9

I

invitations 8
   bluebirds-of-happiness 13
      templates 113

J

jeweled shoe clips 70–1
jeweled-heart greeting card 12

K

keepsake box 106–7
   template 119

L

lace-and-bead heart-shaped sachet
   30–1
lace-edged handkerchief 40–1
lace-trimmed Victorian cornucopia
   54–5
lacy coat hanger 18–19
   template 113
lavender bag 102–3
   template 124
lazy daisy stitch 112
LeMoyne star sachet 102–3
   template 124
love-birds pillow 32–3
   templates 118

N

napkin ring 92–3
nightdress case:
   sweet dreams 36–7
      template 115
note paper, thank-you paper 13

O

over stitch 111

P

photograph album, albums of love
   14–15
photograph frame 98–9

photographer, booking 8
picture of happiness 98–9
pillows:
   love-birds 32–3
      templates 118
   ring 68–9
      template 124
pincushion:
   token of love 34–5
      templates 117
place card:
   bird-of-paradise 13
      template 113
place settings 92–3
posy hair decoration 48–9

R

reception, arranging 7
ring bearer, bow tie and
   cummerbund for 60–1
ring pillow 68–9
   template 124
romantic ring pillow 68–9
   template 124
rose confetti box 86–7
   templates 125
rose and organza box 22
rouleaux 110

S

sachets:
   flowers and herbs 30–1
      template 113
   lavender 102–3
      template 124
sampler 28–9
   template 116
sewing kit 110
sewing stitches 111
sewing techniques 110–11
shells and bells box 25
shoe bag, drawstring 104–5
   templates 123
shoe clips, jeweled 70–1
single hems 111
slip stitch 111
slippers, satin 56–7
souvenir tray 108–9

split stitch 112
stab stitch 111
stitches:
   embroidery 112
   sewing 111
sweet dreams 36–7
   template 115
sweetheart sachet 30–1
   template 113

T

table centerpiece, floral 88–9
tablecloth, for wedding cake 94–5
techniques 110–12
teddy bear's brocade vest 62–3
   templates 123
templates 113–25
thank-you letters 9
thank-you paper 13
tiara 74–5
   template 113
token of affection 40–1
token of love 34–5
   templates 117
transportation 8
tray, découpage souvenir 108–9
trousseau 27

V

vests:
   brocade, for teddy bear 62–3
      templates 123
   for groom 66–7
Victorian cornucopia 54–5

W

web, fusible 111
wedding:
   countdown to 7–9
   planning 6
wedding cake 9
   tablecloth for 94–5
wedding dress 8
   storing 9, 100–1
wedding dress box 100–1
wedding-bells greeting card 12
   template 113

127

Credits

The author wishes to thank everybody who played a part in creating this book, particularly the editorial and design teams at Quarto who made it all possible: Michelle and Pippa who gave such invaluable encouragement throughout; Pat for her meticulous copy editing; Moira, Liz, and Julie for their creativity; and David and Ian who took the pictures.

Special thanks must go to Isabel, Cheryl, and Dorothy for bringing their usual inspiration and friendship to the project, to Terry and Carolyn for their contributions, and also to Christine Kingdom at Offray for her continuing enthusiasm.

Finally, a big thank you to my sister Emma for her imaginative ideas, to my parents Mary and Colin for always being there, and to Jonathan for his love and support. I would like to dedicate this book to the memory of my grandmother, Hilda Griffiths, who taught me to sew.

We would like to thank the designers who designed and made the following projects:

Terry Evans – Hat trick & For the groom
Carolyn Murdoch – Elegant tiara, Crowning glory, Everlasting bouquet & Picture of happiness
Cheryl Owen – Lasting impressions, Albums of love, Gorgeous gifts & Wedding dress box
Isabel Stanley – Love-birds pillow, Beaded hat pin, Jeweled shoe clips, Rose confetti box & LeMoyne star sachet
Dorothy Wood – Box of delights, Heirloom sampler, Posy hair decoration, Beautiful doll & Bridal bag
Lucinda Ganderton – Lacy coat hanger, Beauty basket, Sweetheart sachet, A token of love, Sweet dreams, A token of affection, Victorian cornucopia, Cinderella slippers, Circlet of flowers, Ring bearer style, Bear essentials, Romantic ring pillow, Good luck garter, Center of attention, Bonbonières, Perfect place settings, Wedding cake tablecloth, Drawstring shoe bag, Keepsake box & Découpage souvenir tray

We would also like to acknowledge and thank C.M. Offray & Son Ltd for supplying all of the ribbons used in the projects, and to Bogod Machine Co. for lending the sewing machine featured in the photographs.

C.M. Offray & Son Ltd
Fir Tree Place
Church Road
Ashford
Middlesex TW15 2PH
Tel: (UK) 01784 247281

Bogod Machine Co.
50 Great Sutton Street
London EC1V 0JD
Tel: (UK) 0171 253 1198

All photographs are the copyright of Quarto.

Index by Dorothy Frame.